Simply Creative Quilts

Copyright© 2012 by Leisure Arts, Inc., 5701 Ranch Drive, Little Rock, Arkansas 72223-9633. 501-868-8800, www.leisurearts.com. All rights reserved.

This publication is protected under federal copyright laws. Reproduction or distribution of this publication or any other Leisure Arts publication, including publications which are out of print, is prohibited unless specifically authorized. This includes, but is not limited to, any form of reproduction or distribution on or through the Internet, including posting, scanning, or e-mail transmission. We have made every effort to ensure that these instructions are accurate and complete. We cannot, however, be responsible for human error, typographical mistakes, or variations in individual work.

President and Chief Executive Officer: Rick Barton
Vice President of Sales: Mike Behar
Director of Finance and Administration: Laticia Mull Dittrich
National Sales Director: Martha Adams
Creative Services: Chaska Lucas
Information Technology Director: Hermine Linz
Controller: Francis Caple
Vice President, Operations: Jim Dittrich
Retail Customer Service Manager: Stan Raynor
Print Production Manager: Fred F. Pruss
Vice President and Editor-in-Chief: Susan White Sullivan
Director of Designer Relations: Cheryl Johnson
Special Projects Director: Susan Frantz Wiles
Art Publications Director: Rhonda Shelby
Senior Prepress Director: Mark Hawkins

Produced for Leisure Arts, Inc. by Penn Publishing Ltd.
www.penn.co.il
Editor-in-Chief: Rachel Penn
Editors: Shoshana Brickman, Shula Neufeld
Technical editor: Tamara Bostwick
Design and layout: Ariane Rybski
Photography: Ran Erde

PRINTED IN CHINA

ISBN-13: 978-1-60900-337-1
Library of Congress Control Number: 2011935916

Cover photography by Ran Erde

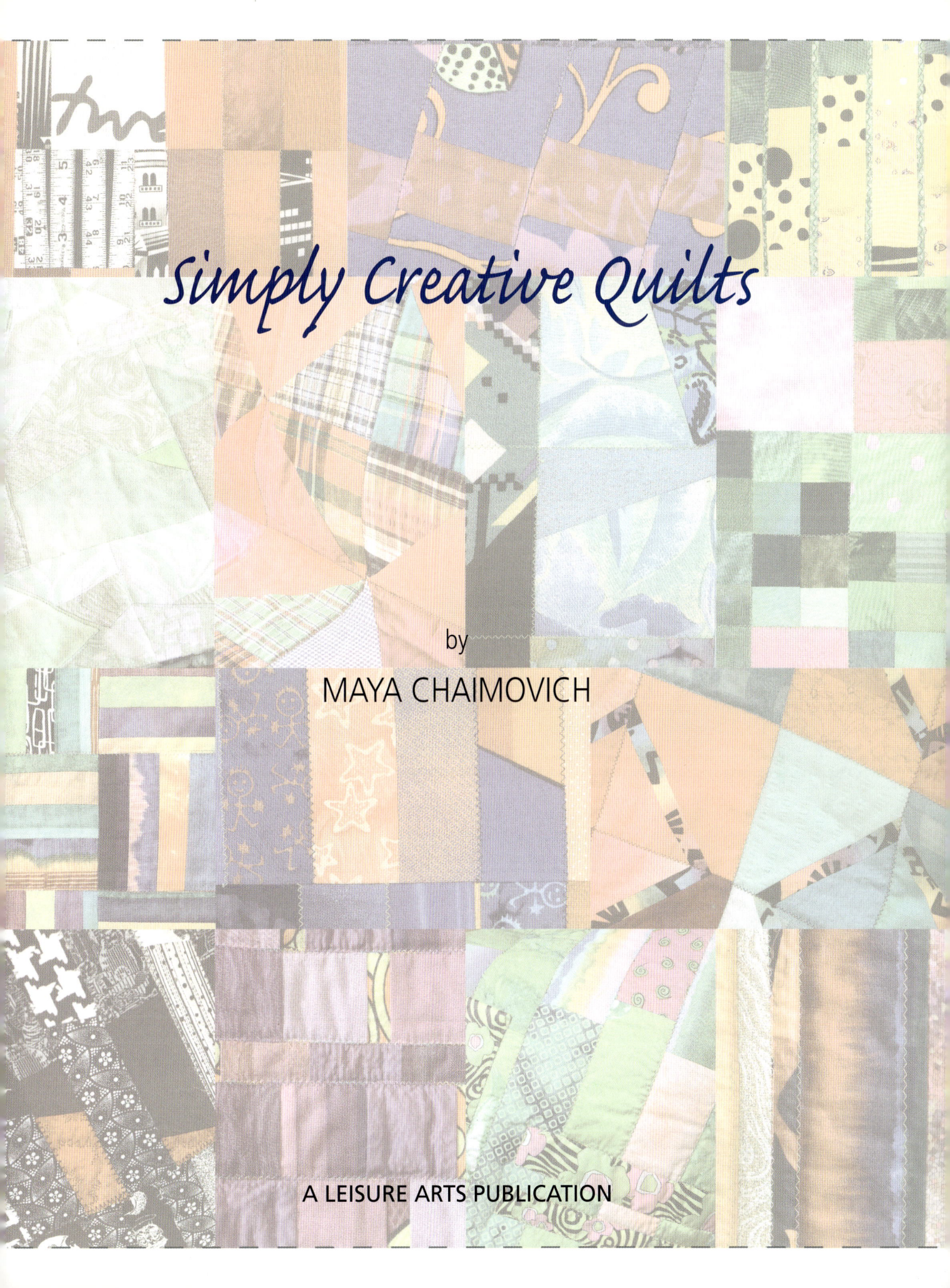

Simply Creative Quilts

by
MAYA CHAIMOVICH

A LEISURE ARTS PUBLICATION

Contents

INTRODUCTION	**6**
Desert Stained Glass	8
Language & Music Quilt	13
Midnight Rose	17
Memory Lane Album Cover	22
Citrus Sassafras	26
Vibrant Window Valance	30
Fuchsia Forest Medley	36
Azure Wonder	40
Golden Age Pillow Covers	45
Quilt of Many Colors	50
Charming Chair Cushions	56
Practical Blanket Pillow	62
Gorgeous Garden Apron	69
Handy Hip Handbag	75
Practical Chair Pockets	80
GENERAL INSTRUCTIONS	**86**
Meet the Designer	96
Metric Conversion Chart	96

Introduction

For me, quilting is a labor of love that comes together as I work on it. I never plan my quilts in advance, but allow them to develop, grow and blossom as I work. More often than not, the idea for my next quilt comes to me as I am working on a different quilt, and that idea is nurtured as I continue to work.

When creating a quilt, I try to integrate as much variety as possible and create a work that is both interesting and beautiful. Often, I strive to combine contrasting elements in every quilt, so that a single work features a variety of colors, diverse patterns, and prints that are of diverse sizes. When cutting the pieces of fabric for each quilt, I frequently cut them in different widths and lengths, to further increase the variety.

I love to use a variety of fabrics in every quilt and I typically choose the exact fabrics that I use as I go along, and suggest you do the same. In other words, use the indicated fabric quantities in these projects as a guideline, but allow yourself to be flexible. More often than not, integrating unexpected elements is what makes a quilt interesting and distinct.

Let your thread color contribute to the final impression of your quilt as well. When working on bright color themes, I find that using multicolored thread can enhance the overall effect.

It is my hope that the projects in this book will inspire you to create quilts that suit your distinct style and taste. Change the sizes, fabric selection, and colors as you like, and leave yourself open to change and alterations. Remember, when it comes to quilting, the possibilities are very literally endless.

Maya Chaimovich

Desert Stained Glass

This striking wall hanging features three rows of lively orange and blue fabrics assembled in a manner that is reminiscent of a glorious desert sunset. I chose both solid and patterned fabrics in each color and sprinkled in a few bright multicolored pieces for contrast. The fabrics evoke the sun, sand and sky — three natural elements that both harmonize and contrast with each other.

DIMENSIONS

* **Finished Quilt Size:** 24½" x 36½" (62cm x 93cm)

MATERIALS

Note If using scraps, you will need pieces that are at least 2¼" x 8½" (6cm x 21cm) to cut the strips.

* ⅝ yard (57cm) assorted blue prints and solids
* ⅝ yard (57cm) assorted orange prints and solids
* ⅛ yard (11cm) piece of patterned multicolored fabric
* ⅞ yard (80cm) of patterned orange fabric for backing
* ¼ yard (23cm) of matching orange fabric for binding

BATTING

* 28½" x 40½" (72cm x 103cm)

YOU WILL ALSO NEED

* Yellow thread
* Multicolored black with metallic green thread

CUTTING

* Follow Rotary Cutting (page 87) to cut fabric. All measurements include ¼" (0.6cm) seam allowances.

FROM BLUE FABRICS

* Cut 29 wide strips 2¼" x 8½" (6cm x 21cm) each

FROM ORANGE FABRICS

* Cut 29 wide strips 2¼" x 8½" (6cm x 21cm) each
* Cut 6 narrow strips 1" x 8½" (2.5cm x 21cm) each

FROM PATTERNED MULTICOLORED FABRIC

* Cut 3 wide strips 2¼" x 8½" (6cm x 21cm) each

FROM BACKING FABRIC

* Cut 1 piece 28½" x 40½" (72cm x 103cm)

FROM ORANGE FABRIC FOR BINDING

* Cut 2 strips 1¾" x 27½" (4.5cm x 70cm) each
* Cut 2 strips 1¾" x 39½" (4.5cm x 100cm) each

Assembling the Quilt Top

Follow directions for Machine Piecing (page 88) and Pressing (page 89) to sew pieces together as described below.

1. Arrange the wide blue and orange strips into 3 rows, each with 19 so that the orange and blue strips are at opposite ends of the rows. Place a few blue strips among the orange for contrast. (Fig. 1)

Fig. 1

2. To make blue and orange sets: Select 2 wide blue strips and 1 narrow orange strip. Place the orange strip between the blue strips, match the long edges and sew together. Repeat to make 6 sets and intersperse along the rows so that there are 2 sets in each row. (Fig. 2)

Fig. 2

3. Sprinkle in the wide strips of patterned multicolored fabric among the orange strips in each of the rows so each row has 20 wide strips. (Fig. 3)

Fig. 3

Fig. 4

4. When satisfied with the overall arrangement of the sets and the strips, sew them together, 5 strips to a group, matching the long edges. Sew the seams in opposite directions to avoid distortion. (Fig. 4)

5. Sew 4 groups of 5 strips together to create a row. Repeat to create 2 more rows. Sew the 3 rows together to complete your quilt top.

Completing the Quilt

Follow Quilting (page 90) to mark, layer and complete the quilted wall hanging.

1. Use a zigzag stitch to quilt along the seams between the strips. For a colorful accent, alternate between the black and yellow threads.

Follow Binding (page 94) to make a binding and sew it to your quilt.

Language & Music Quilt

This design is both striking and rich in meaning. Black on white printed fabrics are combined with bold solid red fabrics. The black and white elements feature diverse written texts including words, music, measurements and art deco images that contrast with the the red fabrics.

DIMENSIONS

* Finished Quilt Size: 24½" x 28¾" (62cm x 73cm)

MATERIALS

Note If using scraps, check the individual descriptions for minimum sizes of scraps needed.

* ⅜ yard (34cm) assorted solid dark red fabrics (scraps need to be at least 2½" x 9" (6cm x 23cm))
* ⅜ yard (34cm) assorted solid light red fabrics (scraps need to be at least 2½" x 9" (6cm x 23cm))
* ¼ yard (23cm) assorted black on white fabric featuring texts (scraps need to be at least 4" x 4" (10cm x 10cm))
* ⅛ yard (11cm) assorted black fabric with white designs (scraps need to be at least 1¾" x 12½" (4.5cm x 32cm))
* ⅞ yard (80cm) of patterned pink fabric for backing
* ¼ yard (23cm) of red fabric for binding

BATTING

* 28½" x 32¾" (72cm x 83cm)

YOU WILL ALSO NEED

* Multicolored white and pink thread

CUTTING THE PIECES

* Follow Rotary Cutting (page 87) to cut fabric. All measurements include ¼" (0.6cm) seam allowances.

FROM SOLID DARK RED FABRIC
* Cut 14 long strips 2¼" x 9" (6cm x 23cm) each

FROM SOLID LIGHT RED FABRIC
* Cut 14 long strips 2¼" x 9" (6cm x 23cm) each

FROM BLACK ON WHITE FABRIC FEATURING TEXTS
* Cut 14 squares 4" x 4" (10cm x 10cm) each

FROM BLACK FABRIC WITH WHITE DESIGNS
* Cut 6 narrow strips 1¾" x 12½" (4.5cm x 32cm) each

FROM BACKING FABRIC
* Cut 1 piece 28½" x 32¾" (72cm x 83cm)

FROM RED FABRIC FOR BINDING
* Cut 2 strips 1¾" x 27½" (4.5cm x 70cm) each
* Cut 2 strips 1¾" x 31" (4.5cm x 81cm) each

Assembling the Quilt Top

Follow directions for Machine Piecing (page 88) and Pressing (page 89) to sew pieces together.

1. Arrange a pair of red strips, matching together 1 dark and 1 light strip. Sew together along one long edge. Repeat with the remaining red strips to create 14 rectangle pairs, each composed of 1 dark and 1 light red strip. (Fig. 1)

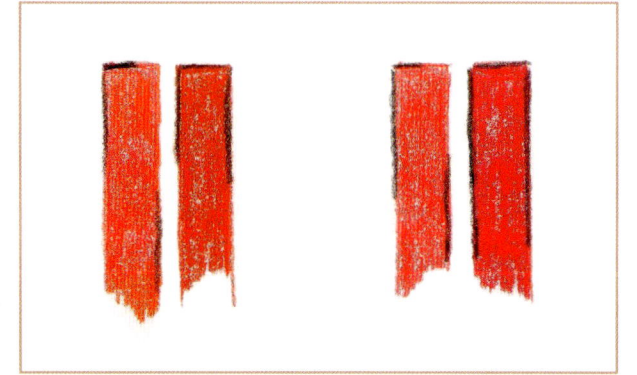

Fig. 1

(continued on page 16)

(continued from page 14)

2. Place 1 black and white square next to a short side of a rectangle and sew together. Repeat to create 14 large rectangles.

3. Arrange the large rectangles into 2 rows, 7 rectangles in each row. Turn some of the rectangles so that the black and white square faces the middle of the quilt, and other rectangles in the opposite direction. (Fig. 3)

Fig. 3

4. Scatter the narrow strips of black fabric with white designs among the 14 rectangles.

5. When satisfied with the arrangement of the strips, sew together the strips of 1 row. Sew seams in opposite directions to avoid distortion. Repeat with the other row. Sew the 2 rows together to create your quilt top. (Fig. 5)

Fig. 5

Completing the Quilt

Follow Quilting (page 90) to mark, layer and complete the quilted wall hanging.

1. Quilt a zigzag stitch along the seams between the strips.

Follow Binding (page 94) to make a binding and sew it to your quilt.

Midnight Rose

Even relatively simple quilts such as this one can make a striking impression. Placed on a coffee table, kitchen table or dresser top, this quilt transforms an ordinary piece of furniture into a piece of art. For this design, I chose a variety of different fabrics that have common colors and distinct patterns.

DIMENSIONS

* **Finished Quilt Size:** 19½" x 25" (49cm x 63.5cm)

MATERIALS

Note If using scraps, check the individual descriptions for minimum sizes of scraps needed. Yardage totals are estimated.

* ⅛ yard (11cm) of fuchsia fabric
* ⅜ yard (34cm) of dark violet fabric
* ⅛ yard (11cm) of fluorescent floral fabric
* ⅛ yard (11cm) of black and light violet polka dot fabric
* ¾ yard (68.5cm) of green and purple fabric for backing
* ¼ yard (23cm) of violet fabric for binding

BATTING

* 23½" x 29" (60cm x 74cm)

YOU WILL ALSO NEED

* Multicolored bright thread

CUTTING THE PIECES

* Follow Rotary Cutting (page 87) to cut fabric. All measurements include ¼" (0.6cm) seam allowances.

FROM FUCHSIA FABRIC

* Cut 1 long strip 2" x 27" (5cm x 69cm)

FROM DARK VIOLET FABRIC

* Cut 4 long strips 1½" x 19" (4cm x 48cm) each
* Cut 2 long wide strips 3½" x 19" (9cm x 48cm) each
* Cut 2 long wide strips 3½" x 19½"" (9cm x 49.5cm) each

FROM FLUORESCENT FLORAL FABRIC

* Cut 2 long strips 2" x 27" (5cm x 69cm) each

FROM BLACK AND LIGHT VIOLET POLKA DOT FABRIC

* Cut 4 long strips 1¾" x 19" (4cm x 48cm) each

FROM BACKING FABRIC

* Cut 1 piece 23½" x 29" (60cm x 74cm)

FROM VIOLET FABRIC FOR BINDING

* Cut 2 strips 1¾" x 22½" (4.5cm x 57cm) each
* Cut 2 strips 1¾" x 28" (4.5cm x 71cm) each

Assembling the Quilt Top

Follow directions for Machine Piecing (page 88) and Pressing (page 89) to sew pieces together.

1. Place the long fuchsia strip next to a fluorescent strip, match and sew along one long edge. Place the other fluorescent strip along the opposite long side of the fuchsia and sew together in the other direction to avoid distortion. (Fig. 1)

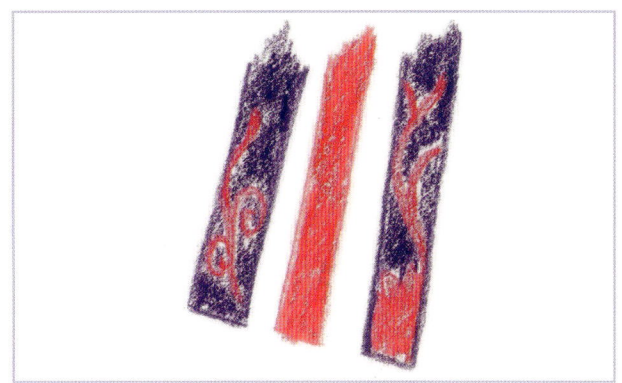
Fig. 1

2. Cut across the piece (opposite to the direction you just sewed) to make 9 pieced strips, each 3" (7.5cm) wide. (Fig. 2)

Fig. 2

3. Arrange the pieced strips in a row, offsetting each strip so that it is ½" (1.3cm) lower than the previous strip. Match the edges and sew the strips together in opposite directions to avoid distortion. (Fig. 3)

4. Turn the assembled block so that the strips you just sewed together are arranged diagonally. Trim off the jagged edges in a straight line along the top, bottom and sides of the piece, creating a 4½" x 19" (11cm x 48cm) rectangle. This is the center block of your quilt. Set aside. (Fig. 4)

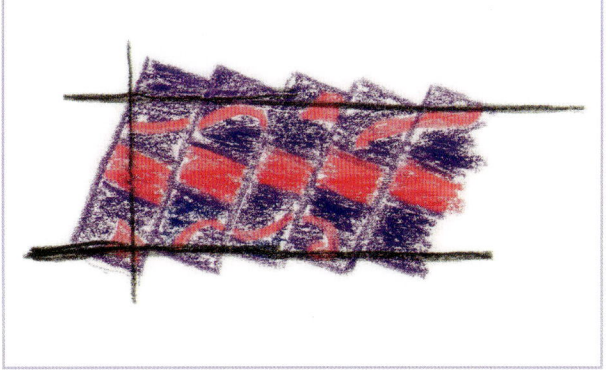
Fig. 3

5. Pair up a long black and violet strip with a long dark violet 1½" (4cm) strip and sew

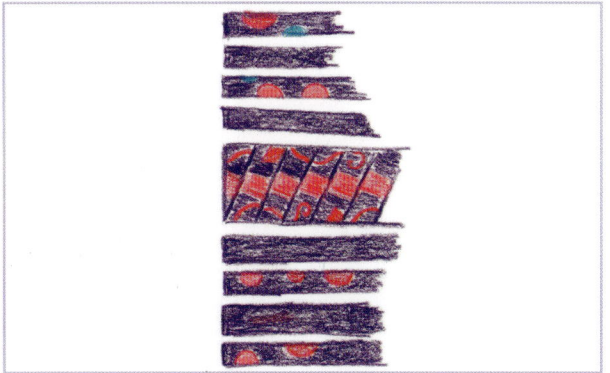
Fig. 4

together along one long edge. Sew another long black and violet strip to the other side of the dark violet strip. Finish the set by sewing a long dark violet strip to the other side of the black and violet strip (sew strips together in opposite directions to prevent distortion). Repeat with the remaining 2 long black and violet strips and long dark violet 1½" (4cm) strips, creating 2 strip sets of 4 long strips each.

6. Sew one of the strip sets to one long edge of the center block. Sew remaining strip set to other side.

7. To finish the quilt top, sew the 19" (48cm) long dark violet wide strips across both the top and bottom of the piece and then sew the 19½" (49.5cm) long wide strips along the sides of the piece.

Completing the Quilt

Follow Quilting (page 90) to mark, layer and complete the quilted wall hanging.

1. Quilt a zigzag stitch with a multicolored thread lengthwise along the rectangle and strips you sewed in steps 6 and 7.

Follow Binding (page 94) to make a binding and sew it to your quilt.

Memory Lane Album Cover

Photo albums are always personalized on the inside. With this project, it's easy to personalize them on the outside too! To make the cover particularly meaningful, select fabrics that remind you of the main theme of the album. For example, if the album holds photos from a recent trip, use fabric from the trip to decorate it!

DIMENSIONS

* **Finished Quilt Size:** 14" x 26" (35.5cm x 66cm) (top) + 3½" (9cm) on each side (7" or 18cm total) folds over to hold album.
* **Finished Strip Sizes:** 4 sizes, ½" to 2¾" x 14" (1cm to 3cm x 35.5cm) wide

YARDAGE REQUIREMENTS

* ¼ yard (23cm) of assorted printed red fabrics
* ¼ yard (23cm) of assorted printed orange fabrics
* ⅜ yard (34cm) of assorted solid red fabrics
* ¼ yard (23cm) of assorted solid orange fabrics
* ⅛ yard (11cm) piece of white with gold fabric
* ½ yard (46cm) of matching colored fabric for backing

BATTING

* 14½" x 33½" (37cm x 85cm)

YOU WILL ALSO NEED

* Multicolored thread to match the fabrics

CUTTING THE PIECES

* Follow Rotary Cutting (page 87) to cut fabric. All measurements include ¼" (0.6cm) seam allowances.

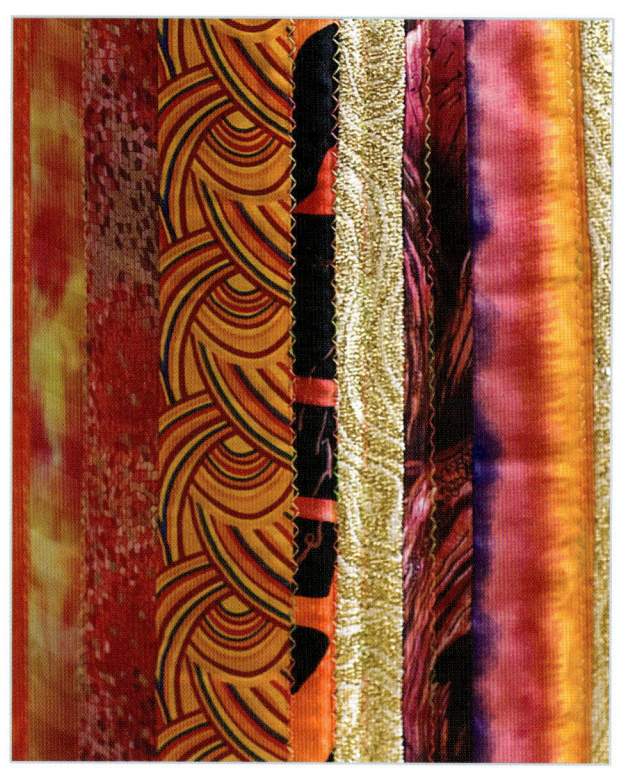

FROM REDS AND ORANGE FABRICS

* Cut 7 narrow strips 1" x 14½" (2.5cm x 37cm) each
* Cut 6 narrow strips 1½" x 14½" (4cm x 37cm) each
* Cut 7 narrow strips 2" x 14½" (5cm x 37cm) each
* Cut 4 strips 3¼" x 14½" (8cm x 37cm) each

FROM WHITE WITH GOLD FABRIC

* Cut 2 narrow strips 1¾" x 14½" (4.5cm x 37cm) each

FROM BACKING FABRIC

* Cut 1 piece 14½" x 33½" (37cm x 85cm)

Assembling the Quilt Top

Follow directions for Machine Piecing (page 88) and Pressing (page 89) to sew pieces together.

1. Arrange the strips of printed and solid red and orange fabrics in a row so that there is an interesting arrangement of colors. Mix in the gold fabric strips near the middle, about 11" (28cm) and 14" (35.5cm) from one end. (Fig. 1)

2. When you are satisfied with the arrangement, match the long edges of the strips and sew them together in opposite

Fig. 1

directions to avoid distortion. The total dimensions of the piece should be 14½" x 33½" (37cm x 85cm). This is your Memory Lane Album Cover quilt top.

Completing the Quilt

Follow Quilting (page 94) to mark, layer and complete the Memory Lane Album Cover.

1. Place the batting on your work surface. Place the quilt top right side up on top of the batting and iron to affix.

2. Place the backing on your work surface, right side up. Place the quilt top with the batting on the backing, right side down. Sew the 3 layers together all around the edges, leaving a 4"(10cm) seam unsewn for turning. Trim the corners. (Fig. 2)

Fig. 2

3. Turn the Album Cover right side out and blindstitch opening closed.

4. Quilt a zigzag stitch along the strips.

5. To finish, make a 3½" (9cm) fold at each end of the Memory Lane Album Cover and sew in place along the top and the bottom. These folds will hold the album front and back in place. (Fig. 3)

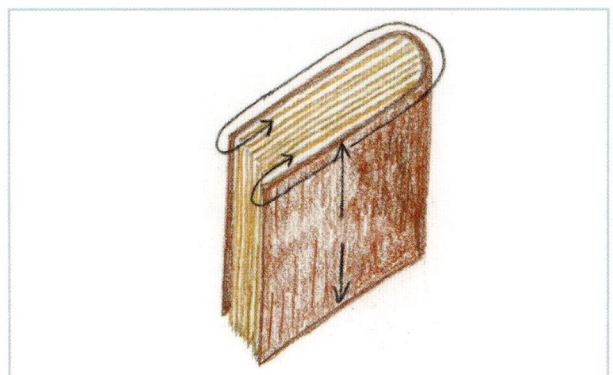

Fig. 3

Citrus Sassafras

This playful wall hanging features bright green and yellow pieces of fabric that are connected in strips and then sewn into long rectangular patches. Cheerful and fun, it's a fantastic project for using up those fabric scraps and is sure to brighten any wall. Add even more color by finishing the quilt with multicolored thread.

DIMENSIONS

* **Finished Quilt Size:** 16½" x 38" (42cm x 97cm)

MATERIALS

Note If using scraps, check the individual descriptions for minimum sizes of scraps needed.

* ⅜ yard (34cm) assorted solid yellow fabrics (scraps need to be at least 3" x 18" (8cm x 46cm))
* ⅜ yard (34cm) assorted patterned yellow fabrics (scraps need to be at least 3" x 18" (8cm x 46cm))
* ⅜ yard (34cm) assorted solid and patterned green fabrics (scraps need to be at least 3" x 18" (8cm x 46cm))
* ¼ yard (23cm) of patterned green and yellow fabric (scraps need to be at least ¾" x 38" (2cm x 97cm))
* ⅝ yard (57cm) of patterned yellow fabric for backing
* ¼ yard (23cm) of yellow and green fabric for binding

BATTING

* 20½" x 42" (52cm x 107cm)

YOU WILL ALSO NEED

* Multicolored black thread with metallic green and yellow

CUTTING THE PIECES

* Follow Rotary Cutting (page 87) to cut fabric. All measurements include ¼" (0.6cm) seam allowances.

FROM SOLID YELLOW AND PATTERNED YELLOW FABRICS

* Cut 10 long strips 3" x 18" (8cm x 46cm) each

FROM SOLID GREEN AND PATTERNED GREEN FABRICS

* Cut 5 long strips 3" x 18" (8cm x 46cm) each

FROM PATTERNED GREEN AND YELLOW FABRIC

* Cut 7 narrow long strips ¾" x 38" (2cm x 97cm) each

FROM BACKING FABRIC

* Cut 1 piece 20½" x 42" (52cm x 107cm)

FROM YELLOW AND GREEN BINDING FABRIC

* Cut 2 strips 1¾" x 41" (4.5cm x 104cm) each
* Cut 2 strips 1¾" x 19½" (4.5cm x 49cm) each

Assembling the Quilt Top

Follow directions for Machine Piecing (page 88) and Pressing (page 89) to sew pieces together.

1. Arrange 15 long strips in a row in the following order: 5 long solid yellow and patterned yellow strips; 5 long solid green and patterned green strips; 5 long solid yellow and patterned yellow strips. (Fig. 1)

Fig. 1

2. When satisfied with the color arrangement, match the edges of the strips and sew them together in opposite directions to avoid distortion. Fold the sewn large piece in half, match the free edges of the first and last strip and sew together, to create a tube. (Fig. 2)

3. Fold the tube flat and cut across it, perpendicular to the strips in 2¼" (6cm) increments. You will end up with 8 narrow tubes.

4. Arrange the 8 tubes in a row, with the green sections in the middle. Adjust each strip at intervals of 1½" (4cm) to create a stepped design using the green sections, first going up toward the middle and then back down.

5. Open the tubes by removing the stitches between 2 sections at the center back of each sleeve to create 8 long strips. Make sure to remove stitches between the correct sections so that the green step design will remain as planned. (Fig. 3)

6. Place a narrow green and yellow strip between each of the 8 long strips. Match the edges along the length of the strips and sew together in opposite directions, to create your quilt top.

Fig. 2

Fig. 3

Completing the Quilt

Follow Quilting (page 90) to mark, layer and complete the quilted wall hanging.

1. Quilt a zigzag stitch using a black with metallic colored thread lengthwise along the 7 narrow green strips.

Follow Binding (page 94) to make a binding and sew it to your quilt.

Vibrant Window Valance

Personalize any window in your home with this vibrant valance featuring vertically and horizontally striped squares. Each square is composed of multiple strips of brightly colored fabric. The colors alternate between light and dark, with no exact pattern, for a random and unpredictable beauty. Every now and then, I've integrated strips of black and white fabric for contrast.

DIMENSIONS

* **Finished Quilt Size:** 14¼" x 39¾" (36cm x 101cm)
* **Finished Block Size:** 4¾" x 4¾" (12cm x 12cm)

MATERIALS

Note If using scraps, check the individual descriptions for minimum sizes of scraps needed.

* ¾ yard (69cm) of assorted dark solid color fabrics (scraps need to be at least 1¼" x 16" (3cm x 40cm)
* ¾ yard (69cm) of assorted light solid color fabrics (scraps need to be at least 1¼" x 16" (3cm x 40cm))
* ⅛ yard (11cm) of black & white fabric (scraps need to be at least 1¼" x 16" (3cm x 40cm)
* ¼ yard (23cm) of multicolored fabric for loops (scraps need to be at least 2" x 8¾" (5cm x 22cm))
* ¼ yard (23cm) of solid matching fabric for border
* ½ yard (46cm) of matching fabric for backing

BATTING

* 14¾" x 40¼" (37cm x 102cm) fusible batting

YOU WILL ALSO NEED

* Multicolored pink, red and yellow thread

CUTTING THE PIECES

* Follow Rotary Cutting (page 87) to cut fabric. All measurements include ¼" (0.6cm) seam allowances.

FROM DARK COLOR FABRIC

* Cut 28 strips 1¼" x 16" (3cm x 40cm) each

FROM LIGHT COLOR FABRIC

* Cut 28 strips 1¼" x 16" (3cm x 40cm) each

FROM BLACK & WHITE FABRIC

* Cut 4 strips 1¼" x 16" (3cm x 40cm) each

FROM MULTICOLORED FABRIC

* Cut 11 loop strips 2" x 8¾" (5cm x 22cm) each

FROM BORDER FABRIC

* Cut 2 strips of 2½" x 18" (6cm x 46cm) each
* Cut 2 strips of 2½" x 42" (6cm x 107cm) each

FROM BACKING FABRIC

* Cut 1 piece 14¾" x 40¼" (37cm x 102cm)

Assembling the Quilt Top

Follow directions for Machine Piecing (page 88) and Pressing (page 89) to sew pieces together.

1. Divide the dark, light, and black & white strips of fabric into 3 sets of 20 strips each. Arrange the strips in each set into rows with alternating patterns of dark and light shades. Consider the shade rather than the color when arranging the strips. (Fig. 1)

Fig. 1

(continued on page 34)

(continued from page 31)

Fig. 2

2. When satisfied with the arrangement, match the long edges of the strips in each row and sew together in opposite directions to avoid distortion. You have created 3 strip sets, each measuring 15½" x 16" (39cm x 40cm).

3. Trimming away any extra fabric, cut each strip set into 9 squares, for a total of 27 squares, each measuring 4¾" x 4¾" (12cm x 12cm).

4. Arrange the squares into 3 rows of 9 squares each. Rotate every other square by 90 degrees, so that the lines of adjacent squares are in alternate directions (horizontal and vertical). (Fig. 2)

5. When satisfied with the arrangement, match the sides of the 3 squares in each vertical row and sew together in opposite directions. Sew the 9 vertical rows of squares together in opposite directions to create a 13¼" x 38¾" (34cm x 97cm) rectangle.

6. Fold each of the 2 long and 2 short narrow strips of border fabric in half lengthwise, right sides facing. Sew together lengthwise.

7. Matching raw edges, sew longer border strips along the top and bottom edges of the rectangle, right sides facing. Repeat along sides using shorter strips to finish your quilt top.

Completing the Quilt

Follow Quilting (page 90) to mark, layer and complete the quilted valance.

1. Make a ¼" (1cm) lengthwise fold along each long side of each narrow strip of multicolored fabric, wrong sides facing and iron. Fold each strip in half lengthwise and sew a long zigzag seam along open edge to secure. These are the 11 loop straps for your valance. (Fig. 3)

2. Place the batting on your work surface. Place the quilt top right side up on top of the batting and iron to affix.

3. Place the backing on your work surface, right side up. Place the quilt top with the batting on top, right side down.

4. Fold each strap sewn in step 1 in half, to form a loop. Tuck each loop between the 2 layers of the quilt at uneven intervals along one long side, the raw ends of each loop flush with the edges. Pin the loop ends to affix. (Fig. 4)

5. Sew all around the quilt, securing the loops as you sew, leaving a 6" (15cm) section at the bottom unsewn.

6. Trim the corners and turn the quilt top right side out.

7. Blindstitch the section along the bottom that was left unsewn.

8. Quilt a zigzag stitch along the seams between the rows. (Fig. 5)

Fig. 3

Fig. 4

Fig. 5

Fuchsia Forest Medley

This wall hanging features a cornucopia of gorgeous green and pink fabrics. It reminds me of fresh tree buds and cherry blossoms, evoking the sights and smells of springtime. Assembling this quilt was a lot like putting together a puzzle. I simply altered the position of the pieces, moving them around and adjusting their orientation, until it was just right.

DIMENSIONS

* **Finished Quilt Size:** 24½" x 30½" (62cm x 77cm)
* **Finished Block Size:** 6½" x 6½" (16cm x 16cm)

MATERIALS

Note If using scraps, check the individual descriptions for minimum sizes of scraps needed.

* 1⅛ yard (103cm) 12 assorted patterned green fabrics to total approximately (scraps need to be at least 2½" x 9½" (6cm x 24.5cm) or 4" x 4" (10cm x 10cm))
* ¼ yard (23cm) 8 different patterned pinks and fuchsia fabrics to total approximately (scraps need to be at least 2" x 4" (5cm x 10cm) with one piece being 7¼" x 7¼" (18.5cm x 18.5cm))
* ⅞ yard (80cm) of pink with green fabric for backing
* ¼ yard (23cm) of green fabric for binding

BATTING

* 28½" x 34½" (72cm x 88cm)

YOU WILL ALSO NEED

* Multicolored bright green and yellow thread

CUTTING THE PIECES

* Follow Rotary Cutting (page 87) to cut fabric. All measurements include ¼" (0.6cm) seam allowances.

FROM PATTERNED GREEN FABRICS

* Cut 48 strips 2" x 8" (5cm x 20cm) each
* Cut 10 squares 3½" x 3½" (9cm x 9cm) each

FROM PATTERNED PINK FABRICS

* Cut 12 squares 3½" x 3½" (9cm x 9cm) each
* Cut 3 rectangles 3½" x 6½" (9cm x 16.5cm) each
* Cut 1 square 6½" x 6½" (16.5cm x 16.5cm)

FROM BACKING FABRIC

* Cut 1 piece 28½" x 34½" (72cm x 88cm)

FROM GREEN BINDING FABRIC

* Cut 2 strips 1¾" x 33½" (4.5cm x 85cm) each
* Cut 2 strips 1¾" x 27½" (4.5cm x 70cm) each

Assembling the Quilt Top

Follow directions for Machine Piecing (page 88) and Pressing (page 89) to sew pieces together.

1. Arrange the 48 strips of green fabrics into 12 groups of 4 strips, so that each group features 4 different types of fabric. (Fig. 1)

2. Matching the long edges of a set of 4 strips, sew together to create a square. Sew seams in opposite directions to avoid distortion. Repeat with the remaining strip sets to make 12 large squares.

Fig. 1

3. Cut across a large square (opposite to the direction you just sewed) to make 4 checkered strips, 2" (5cm) wide. Repeat with the remaining 11 squares to make 48 checkered strips. (Fig. 2)

4. Rearrange all the checkered strips. Sew 4 strips together to make a checkerboard square. Repeat to make 11 squares. Sew 2 strips together to make a checkerboard rectangle. Repeat once to make 2 rectangles. (Fig. 3)

5. Arrange the checkerboard sets with the remaining 3½" x 3½" (9cm x 9cm) pink and green squares, 3½" x 6½" (9cm x 16.5cm) rectangles and 6½" x 6½" (16.5cm x 16.5cm) square until you find an arrangement you like. Sew all pieces together to finish the quilt top.

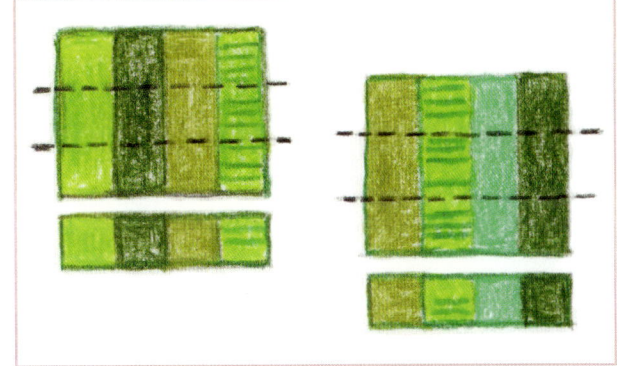

Fig. 2

Fig. 3

Completing the Quilt

Follow Quilting (page 90) to mark, layer and complete the quilted wall hanging.

1. Quilt a zigzag stitch along the seams of the squares. Repeat with some of the small checkered squares to create more variety.

Follow Binding (page 94) to make a binding and sew it to your quilt.

Azure Wonder

In this modern design, squares of dark fabric are integrated with squares of bright blue fabric to create a striking swirled center. The square patches of fabric are comprised of both single fabric pieces and 2-section pieces, creating even more distinction. Each square is a miniature work of art; together, they harmonize to create the wonder of the entire quilt.

DIMENSIONS

* Finished Quilt Size: 27½" x 32" (70cm x 80cm)
* Finished Square Size: 4½" x 4½" (11.5cm x 11.5cm)

MATERIALS

Note If using scraps, check the individual descriptions for minimum sizes of scraps needed. Yardage totals are estimated.

* ⅜ yard (34cm) of printed black fabric
* ¼ yard (23cm) of solid black fabric
* ½ yard (46cm) assorted printed bright blue fabrics (scraps need to be at least 6" x 6" (15cm x 15cm))
* ⅜ yard (34cm) assorted solid bright blue fabrics (scraps need to be at least 6" x 6" (15cm x 15cm))
* 1 yard (91cm) of matching blue fabric for backing
* ¼ yard (23cm) of light blue fabric for binding

BATTING

* 31½" x 36" (80cm x 91cm)

YOU WILL ALSO NEED

* Multicolored bright green and yellow thread

CUTTING THE PIECES

* Follow Rotary Cutting (page 87) to cut fabric. All measurements include ¼" (0.6cm) seam allowances.

FROM PRINTED BLACK FABRIC

* Cut 11 squares 5" x 5" (13cm x 13cm) each

FROM SOLID BLACK FABRIC

* Cut 3 squares 5" x 5" (13cm x 13cm) each

FROM PRINTED AND SOLID BRIGHT BLUE FABRICS

* Cut 18 large squares 6" x 6" (15cm x 15cm) each

FROM PRINTED AND SOLID BRIGHT BLUE FABRICS

* Cut 10 squares 5" x 5" (13cm x 13cm) each

FROM BACKING FABRIC

* Cut 1 piece 31½" x 36" (80cm x 90cm)

FROM LIGHT BLUE BINDING FABRIC

* Cut 2 strips 1¾" x 30½" (4.5cm x 77cm) each
* Cut 2 strips 1¾" x 35" (4.5cm x 89cm) each

Assembling the Quilt Top

Follow directions for Machine Piecing (page 88) and Pressing (page 89) to sew pieces together.

1. Cut across a large blue square on a diagonal that extends from 1¼" (3cm) from one corner to 3¼" (8cm) from the diagonally opposite corner. You have 1 large and 1 small piece of fabric. Repeat with the remaining 17 large blue squares, for a total of 18 large and 18 small pieces. (Fig. 1)

Fig. 1

2. Arrange 1 small and 1 large piece of different fabrics to form a square. Repeat with the remaining cut pieces, mixing fabrics. When satisfied with the arrangement, match the edges and sew together to form 18 new squares. (Fig. 2)

Fig. 2

3. Trim the new squares down to 5" x 5" (13cm x 13cm) to conform in size with the other squares.

4. Arrange a spiral design with the 14 black squares. Continue by placing the remaining blue squares inside and around the spiral. Make sure it is completely surrounded by blue squares. (Fig. 3)

Fig. 3

5. When satisfied with the arrangement, match the edges of the squares in the first row and sew together in opposite directions to avoid distortion. Repeat with the remaining 6 rows.

6. Sew the rows together in opposite directions to finish the quilt top.

Completing the Quilt

Follow Quilting (page 90) to mark, layer and complete the Quilted Wall Hanging.

1. Quilt a zigzag stitch along the vertical and horizontal seams separating the squares and along the diagonal seams joining the pieced squares.

Follow Binding (page 94) to make a binding and sew it to your quilt.

Golden Age Pillow Covers

This pair of pillow covers is an easy way to add a personal touch to your bedroom without creating a complete quilt. Made primarily of black and white patterned fabrics, the covers contain a few carefully positioned strips of orange fabric to make things a bit more interesting. The overall effect reminds me a bit of a black & white movie—lots of glamour and excitement, with a touch of earthiness that sets it all off. The quilting was done using black and white threads.

DIMENSIONS

* **Finished Quilt Size:** 21" x 21" (53.5cm x 53.5cm) each pillow

MATERIALS

* ½ yard (46cm) of solid white fabric (scraps need to be at least 9" x 9" (23cm x 23cm)
* ½ yard (46cm) of solid black fabric (scraps need to be at least 9" x 9" (23cm x 23cm)
* ½ yard (46 cm) of assorted white and black printed fabrics (scraps need to be at least 9" x 9" (23cm x 23cm))
* ⅜ yard (34cm) of orange fabric (scraps need to be at least 9" x 9" (23cm x 23cm)
* 1⅜ yards (125cm) of fabric for backing
* 1⅜ yards (125cm) of thick cream color fabric for pillow covers

BATTING

* 2 pieces fusible batting, 23" x 23" (58.5cm x 58.5cm) each

YOU WILL ALSO NEED

* 2 pieces, 23" x 23" (58.5cm x 58.5cm) each, of fusible interfacing
* Black and white threads

CUTTING THE PIECES

* Follow Rotary Cutting (page 87) to cut fabric. All measurements include ¼" (0.6cm) seam allowances.

FROM SOLID WHITE FABRIC
* Cut 6 squares 9" x 9" (23cm x 23cm) each

FROM SOLID BLACK FABRIC
* Cut 6 squares 9" x 9" (23cm x 23cm) each

FROM WHITE AND BLACK FABRICS
* Cut 8 squares 9" x 9" (23cm x 23cm) each

FROM ORANGE FABRIC
* Cut 3 squares 9" x 9" (23cm x 23cm) each

FROM BACKING FABRIC
* Cut 2 pieces, 23" x 23" (58.5cm x 58.5cm) each

FROM CREAM PILLOW COVERING FABRIC
* Cut 4 pieces, 17" x 23" (43cm x 58cm) each

Assembling the Quilt Top

Follow directions for Machine Piecing (page 88) and Pressing (page 89) to sew pieces together.

1. Place a 9" x 9" (23cm x 23cm) fabric square on your work surface and cut it on a diagonal that extends from 2" from one corner to 4" from the diagonally opposite corner. (Fig. 1)

2. Repeat this process to cut all the 9" x 9" (23cm x 23cm) squares into 2 pieces each.

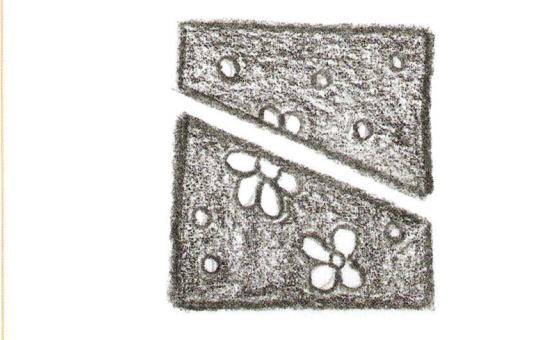

Fig. 1

3. Rearrange all the pieces to make 23 new squares, each of them made from 2 different pieces of fabric that are different in color.

4. Sew the matched pieces together to create new squares. Trim the squares so each square is 8" x 8" (20.5cm x 20.5cm.)

5. Place 1 two-color square on your work surface and cut it into 4 strips, 2" (5cm) each. (Fig. 2)

6. Repeat step 5 to cut all the two-color squares into 2" (5cm) strips. Divide the strips at random into 2 sets, 45 strips to a strip set.

7. Place one 23" x 23" (58.5cm x 58.5cm) piece of fusible interfacing fabric on your work surface. Arrange all the pieces of 1 strip set, right side up, on top of the fusible interfacing. Position them to make 3 rows. Make sure the strips overlap each other by about ¼" (6mm) on each side. Play with the design until you are happy with the composition. Iron the strips onto the interfacing fabric to adhere them in place. Trim any pieces that overlap the edges of the fusible interfacing. (Fig. 3)

8. Place the other piece of interfacing fabric on your worktable and repeat step 7 to attach the other strip set.

Fig. 2

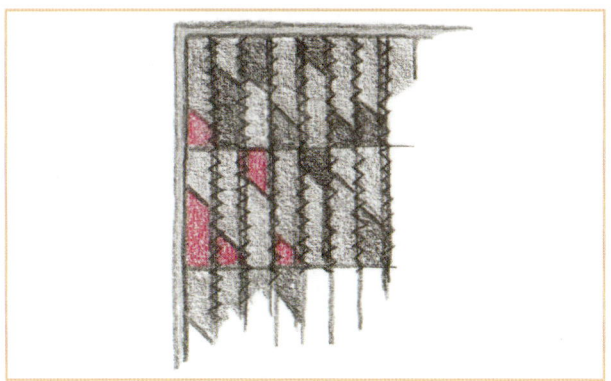

Fig. 3

Completing the Quilt

Follow Quilting (page 90) to mark, layer and complete each quilt top.

1. Quilt both quilt tops with a zigzag stitch. Sew along the sides and between the strips, alternating with black and white threads.

2. Place batting piece on your ironing board. Place quilt top right side up on the batting piece and iron. Repeat with the other piece of batting and quilt top.

3. Place a 23" x 23" (58.5cm x 58.5cm) backing piece, right side down, on your work surface. Place 1 quilted quilt top, right side up, on top of the backing. Sew the layers together on all 4 sides.

4. Repeat with the other backing piece and quilt top.

5. Finish one long edge of each of the pillow cover pieces by turning the raw edge over by ¼" (0.6cm) twice and sew to secure.

6. Lay one quilt top on your surface with the right side up. Place 2 pillow cover pieces on top, right sides down so that the raw edges are even with the outside edges of the pillow cover top and overlap by about 10" (25.5cm) inches in the center (the finished edges of the pillow cover pieces should be placed in the middle). Pin all edges in place. (Fig. 4)

7. Sew around the 4 outer edges of the pillow using a ½" (1cm) seam allowance. The overlapping of the pillow cover sections creates an opening for inserting a pillow.

8. Turn the pillow cover right-side out to finish. Repeat steps 5 and 6 to make the other Golden Age Pillow Cover.

Fig. 4

Quilt of Many Colors

For this quilt, I worked with two groups of fabrics with contrasting colors. One group features solid red fabrics and the other group features plaid and checkered fabrics in a wide range of colors. This quilt can cover a single bed or be used as a couch throw for an attractive decoration. Because of the wide range of colors, it's suited for almost every type of room and guaranteed to add life and color.

DIMENSIONS

* **Finished Quilt Size:** 52 ½" x 65 ½" (133cm x 165cm)
Finished Small Block Size: 7" x 7" (18cm x 18cm)
* **Finished Large Block Size:** 13 ½" x 13 ½ (34cm x 34cm)

YARDAGE REQUIREMENTS

* 2 yards (182cm) of assorted red fabrics
* 2 yards (182cm) of assorted plaid and checkered fabrics
* 1 ¾ yards (160cm) of matching 90" (229cm) wide fabric for backing
* ½ yard (46cm) of matching fabric for binding

BATTING

* 60 ½" x 73 ½" (154cm x 187cm)

YOU WILL ALSO NEED

* Multicolored black with metallic red thread

CUTTING THE PIECES

* Follow Rotary Cutting (page 87) to cut fabric. All measurements include ¼" (0.6cm) seam allowances.

FROM RED FABRICS

* Cut 40 squares 8" x 8" (20cm x 20cm) each

FROM PLAID AND CHECKERED FABRICS

* Cut 40 squares 8" x 8" (20cm x 20cm) each

FROM BACKING FABRIC

* Cut piece 60½" x 73½" (154cm x 187cm)

FROM BINDING FABRIC

Cut seven 1¾" x 40" (4.5cm x 102cm) strips and piece them together to create:
* 2 strips 1¾" x 55½" (4.5cm x 141cm) each
* 2 strips 1¾" x 68½" (4.5cm x 174cm) each

Assembling the Quilt Top

Follow directions for Machine Piecing (page 88) and Pressing (page 89) to sew pieces together.

1. Place 1 red fabric square and 1 plaid fabric square together, right sides facing. Pin the squares together in the corners to hold them together. Iron the 2 squares together to compress. (Figs. 1-2)

2. Draw a diagonal line between 2 opposite corners across the middle of 1 square. Pin fabrics together on each side of the line.

3. Sew 2 seams along the diagonal line you drew in step 2, 1 seam on each side of the line. (Fig. 3)

4. Cut the square into 2 equal triangles by cutting on the line between the diagonal seams. Open the triangles. You have created 2 new squares, each with a diagonal seam across the center, connecting 1 solid and 1 plaid triangle. (Fig. 4)

Fig. 1

Fig. 2

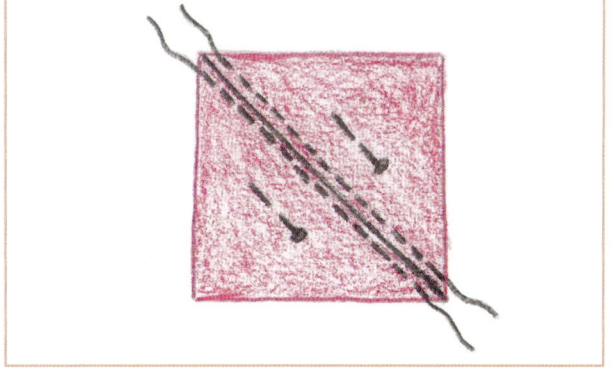
Fig. 3

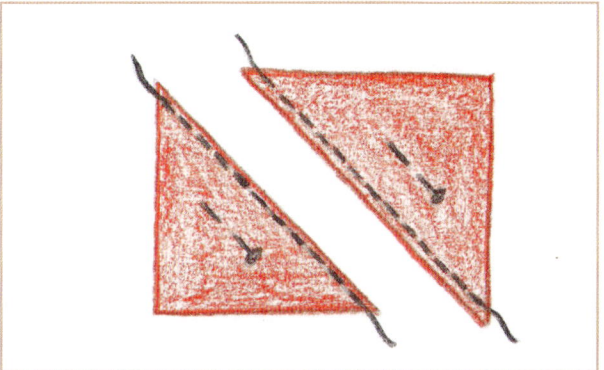
Fig. 4

5. Repeat steps 1—4 with the remaining squares, to make 80 new squares. Make sure each new square has 1 solid and 1 plaid, or 1 solid and 1 checkered triangle. Trim squares down to 7" x 7" (18cm x 18cm). (Fig. 5)

6. Join a pair of squares together, making sure that each square in the pair has a different printed fabric. Sew the squares together via the printed sides of each square to make a rectangle.

7. Repeat step 6 with the remaining pairs of squares to make 40 rectangles. Each rectangle should feature one large printed triangle in the middle, and 1 smaller red triangle at each side.

8. Join a pair of rectangles together to create a large square featuring a diamond in the middle, made from 4 different printed triangles. The red triangles should be at the corners of the square. (Fig. 6)

9. Repeat step 8 with the remaining rectangles to make 20 large squares.

10. Arrange all 20 large squares to make 5 rows of 4 squares each. When you are satisfied with the arrangement, join the squares in the first row together and sew in opposite directions to avoid distortion.

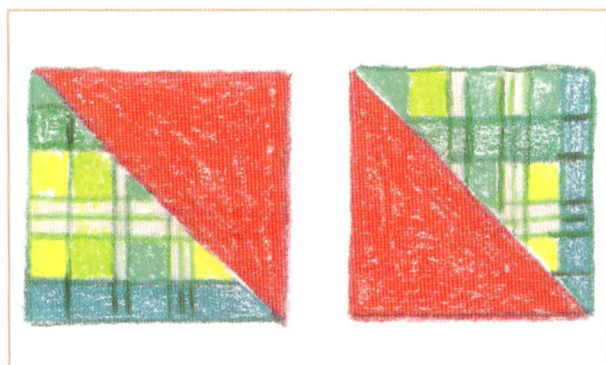

Fig. 5

Fig. 6

Repeat and join the squares in the remaining rows. Now join the rows and sew them together to finish your quilt top.

Completing the Quilt

Follow Quilting (page 90) to mark, layer and complete the quilt.

1. Since this is a large quilt, you should baste the 3 layers together to secure before quilting. Place the 3 layers on your work surface, backing side on top. Hand baste large stitches horizontally and diagonally, moving from the center toward the outer edges to avoid distortion.

2. Quilt a zigzag stitch along the seams of the small squares to outline them. Sew horizontally and diagonally, moving from the center toward the outer edges to avoid distortion. Remove basting stitches.

Follow Binding (page 94) to make a binding and sew it to your quilt.

Charming Chair Cushions

This set of pretty chair covers can be made for one special chair or an entire set. It's perfect for giving a favorite old chair an entirely new look, and is a great way of adding vibrant color to ordinary furniture. If the chair you want to dress up seems a bit larger or smaller than average, measure the chair back and base and adjust your final quilt size accordingly.

DIMENSIONS

* **Finished Back Cushion Size:** 13½" x 16" (34cm x 41cm)
* **Finished Bottom Cushion Size:** 15" x 16¼" (38cm x 41cm)

YARDAGE REQUIREMENTS

Quantities noted will make one cushion, multiply according to how many cushions you wish to make.

* ⅜ yard (34cm) of assorted dark purple fabrics (scraps need to be at least 2¾" x 19½" (7cm x 49cm))
* ⅜ yard (34cm) of assorted light purple fabrics (scraps need to be at least 2¾" x 19½" (7cm x 49cm))
* ⅛ yard (11cm) of vibrant colored fabric (scraps need to be at least 1¾" x 19½" (4.5cm x 49cm))
* ⅝ yard (57cm) of solid purple fabric for backing
* ⅜ yard (34cm) of dark purple fabric for binding and straps
* ⅛ yard (11cm) of vibrant fabric for binding

BATTING

* Back cushion, 17½" x 20" (44cm x 51cm)
* Bottom cushion, 19" x 20¼" (48cm x 51cm)

YOU WILL ALSO NEED

* Multicolored thread to match the fabrics

CUTTING THE PIECES

* Follow Rotary Cutting (page 87) to cut fabric. All measurements include ¼" (0.6cm) seam allowances.

FROM ASSORTED DARK PURPLE FABRICS

* Cut 4 strips 2" x 19¼" (5cm x 49cm) each, for Bottom Cushion
* Cut 4 strips 2" x 16½" (5cm x 42cm) each, for Back Cushion

FROM ASSORTED LIGHT PURPLE FABRICS

* Cut 4 strips 2" x 19¼" (5cm x 49cm) each, for Bottom Cushion
* Cut 4 strips 2" x 16½" (5cm x 42cm) each, for Back Cushion

FROM VIBRANT COLORED FABRIC

* Cut 2 narrow strips 1" x 19¼" (2.5cm x 49cm) each, for Bottom Cushion
* Cut 2 narrow strips 1" x 16½" (2.5cm x 42cm) each, for Back Cushion
* Cut 2 narrow strips 1¼" x 16¼" (3cm x 41cm) each, for Bottom Cushion
* Cut 2 narrow strips 1½" x 13½" (4cm x 34cm) each, for Back Cushion
* Cut 2 narrow strips 1¾ x 18" (4.5cm x 46cm) each, for bottom binding
* Cut 2 narrow strips 1¾" x 19¼" (4.5cm x 49cm) each, for bottom binding

FROM DARK PURPLE BINDING/ STRAP FABRIC

* Cut 2 narrow strips 1¾" x 16½" (4.5cm x 42cm) each, for back binding
* Cut 2 narrow strips 1¾" x 19" (4.5cm x 48cm) each, for back binding
* Cut 8 ribbon strips 1¾" x 19" (4.5cm x 48cm) each, for straps

FROM SOLID PURPLE BACKING FABRIC

* Cut 1 piece 17½" x 20" (44cm x 51cm) for Back Cushion
* Cut 1 piece 19" x 20" (48cm x 51cm) for Bottom Cushion

Assembling the Quilt Top

Follow directions for Machine Piecing (page 88) and Pressing (page 89) to sew pieces together.

To Make the Back Cushion (use 16½" strips)

1. Arrange 4 strips of dark and 4 strips of light purple fabric in alternating order and sprinkle in 2 narrow strips of vibrant colored fabric. (Fig. 1)

2. Sew the strips together in opposite directions to avoid distortion.

3. Cut across the strip set (opposite to the direction you just sewed) to make 5 new strips, each 2¾"x 15½" (7cm x 39cm) wide and 2 strips, each 1⅜" x 15½" (3.5cm x 39cm). (Fig. 2)

4. Arrange all the new strips, alternating the order of dark and light fabrics. When satisfied with the arrangement, match the long edges of the strips in each row and sew together in opposite directions alternating wide and narrow strip sets.

5. Sew a narrow strip of vibrant fabric, 1½" x 13½" (4cm x 34cm), along each side of the piece, to frame the sides of your Back Cushion.

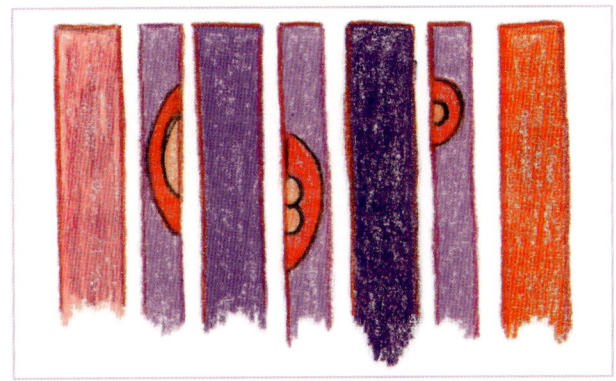

Fig. 1

Fig. 2

To make the Bottom Cushion (use 19¼" strips)

6. Repeat steps 1 and 2.

7. Cut across the strip set (opposite the direction you just sewed) to make 7 new strips, each 2¾" x 19¼" (7cm x 49cm) wide.

8. Repeat step 4.

9. Sew a narrow strip of vibrant fabric, 1 1¼" x 16¼" (3cm x 41cm), along each side of the piece, to frame the sides of your Bottom Cushion.

To Make the Straps

10. Make a ¼" (1cm) lengthwise fold along each long side of each dark purple strap, wrong sides facing. Fold the strap in half lengthwise, folds (hems) tucked in. Iron and sew along length of strap to secure. Repeat with the remaining 7 straps.

Completing the Quilt

Follow Quilting (page 90) to mark, layer and complete the quilted cushions.

1. Quilt a zigzag stitch along the seams between the strips of the back cushion.

2. Quilt a zigzag stitch along the seams between the strips of the seat cushion.

Follow Binding (page 94) to make a binding. Do not sew the binding to the backing.

1. Leaving the corners unsewn, sew the dark purple binding strips to Back Cushion. Repeat with vibrant colored binding strips for the Seat Cushion.

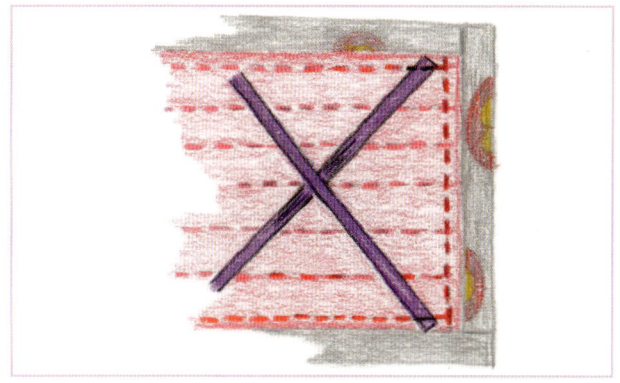

Fig. 3

2. Insert 1 strap end on a diagonal at each corner of each pillow, tucked between the binding and backing. (Fig. 3)

3. Fold unsewn sections of binding strips over the strap ends and onto cushion backing, pin in place to affix.

4. Blindstitch the binding to the backing, making sure to secure the straps in place.

5. Fold in the raw strap ends and blindstitch to secure. Your set of cushions is complete.

Practical Blanket Pillow

This easy-to-make project is perfect for people who love to curl up by the TV. It's a small quilted blanket that folds up tidily into its very own pillow pocket. For this quilt, I chose a number of red fabrics, patterned turquoise fabrics, and one black fabric with colored designs. The pillow pocket quilted top is made from a piece of rainbow tie-dyed fabric and the lining is a lovely shade of turquoise.

DIMENSIONS

* **Finished Quilt Size:** 32½" x 42½" (83cm x 108cm)
* **Pocket Pillow Size:** 13½" x 13½" (34cm x 34cm)
* **Small Block Size:** 5½" x 5½" (14cm x14cm)
* **Large Block Size:** 10½" x 10½" (27cm x 27cm)

MATERIALS

* ¾ yard (69cm) of 12 assorted red fabrics (scraps need to be at least 6" x 6" (15cm x 15cm))
* ¾ yard (69cm) of 12 assorted turquoise fabrics (scraps need to be at least 6" x 6" (15cm x 15cm))
* ⅜ yard (34cm) of black print fabric (scraps need to be at least 1¼" x 7" (3cm x 18cm))
* ¼ yard (23cm) of solid turquoise green fabric for border
* ½ yard (46cm)(or fat quarter) of matching colorful fabric for pocket
* ½ yard (46cm)(or fat quarter) of turquoise green fabric for lining of pocket
* 1⅛ yards (103cm) of matching fabric for quilt backing
* ½ yard (46cm)(or fat quarter) of matching fabric for pocket backing

BATTING

* Fusible batting for quilt, 36½" x 44½" (93cm x 1113cm)
* Fusible batting for pocket, 16" x 16" (41cm x 41cm)

YOU WILL ALSO NEED

* Turquoise thread
* Multicolored black with metallic red thread

CUTTING THE PIECES

* Follow Rotary Cutting (page 87) to cut fabric. All measurements include ¼" (0.6cm) seam allowances.

FROM RED FABRICS
* Cut 24 squares 6" x 6" (15cm x 15cm) each

FROM TURQUOISE FABRICS
* Cut 24 squares 6" x 6" (15cm x 15cm) each

FROM BLACK PRINT FABRIC
* Cut 48 strips 1¼" x 7" (3cm x 18cm) each

FROM MATCHING COLORFUL FABRIC
* Cut one 14" x 14" (35.5cm x 35.5cm) square for pocket

FROM MATCHING SOLID TURQUOISE GREEN FABRIC
* Cut 2 long strips 1½" x 43" (4cm x 109cm) each and
* 2 long strips 1½" x 35" (3cm x 89cm) each, for borders
* Cut 14½" x 16½" (37cm x 42cm) for pocket lining
* Cut 2" x 14" (5cm x 35.5cm) strip for pocket lining

FROM BACKING FABRIC
* Cut 14½" x 16½" (37cm x 42cm) for back of pocket
* Cut one 16" x 16" (41cm x 41cm) square for pocket lining

Assembling the Quilt Top

Follow directions for Machine Piecing (page 88) and Pressing (page 89) to sew pieces together.

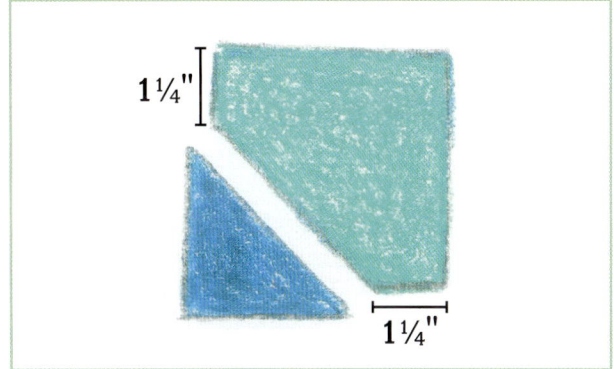

Fig. 1

1. Measure and draw a diagonal line 1¼" (3cm) from opposite corners of a small turquoise square in both directions and cut along the line. You should have a small right-angled triangle with 2 sides measuring 4¾" (12cm) each. Cut along the diagonal line. Repeat and cut small triangles from all the remaining red and turquoise small squares. (Fig. 1)

Fig. 2

2. Select a turquoise triangle and a larger section from a different turquoise fabric. Place a black print strip between the 2 sections and sew seams to join the 3 sections together to create a new square. (Figs. 2-3)

3. Mix and arrange the remaining turquoise green sections and repeat step 2, to make 24 new turquoise squares with a black print strip sewn between the 2 sections of each square.

Fig. 3

4. Mix and arrange the red sections, with 2 different fabrics to a square. Repeat step 2 to make 24 new red squares with a black print strip sewn between the 2 sections of each square. Trim all new squares down to 5½" x 5½" (14cm x14cm).

5. Arrange 4 new red squares to form a large square: Join and sew 2 of the red squares together, then sew the other 2 squares together. Sew the 2 sections together to complete a large 10½" x 10½" (27cm x 27cm) square. (Fig. 4)

6. Arrange the remaining red squares into large squares and repeat step 5 to make 6 large red squares. Repeat with the turquoise squares to make 6 large turquoise squares. You have a total of 12 large blocks.

Fig. 4

7. Arrange and alternate the large red and turquoise green squares into 4 rows of 3 squares in each. When you are satisfied with the arrangement, join the squares in the first row together and sew in opposite directions to avoid distortion. Repeat and join the squares in the remaining rows. Now join the 4 rows and sew them together. (Fig. 5)

Fig. 5

8. Fold the 2 long and 2 short border strips of turquoise green fabric in half lengthwise, wrong sides together. Press.

9. Matching raw edges and right sides together, sew longer border strips along the top and bottom edges of the quilt. Repeat along sides using shorter strips to finish quilt top.

Assembling the Quilt Top Pocket

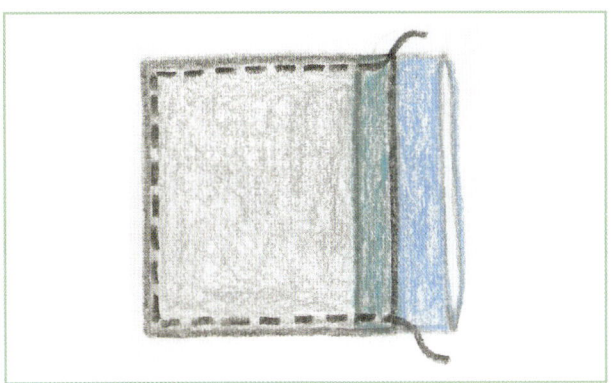

Fig. 6

1. Place the 16" x 16" (41cm x 41cm) piece of batting on your work surface. Place the 16" x 16" (41cm x 41cm) matching colorful fabric square on top of the batting, right side up, and iron to affix.

Follow Quilting (page 90) to mark, layer and complete the Quilt Pocket:

2. Place the 16" x 16" (41cm x 41cm) backing on your work surface, wrong side up. Place the 2-layered quilt top on the backing, right side up, and pin to secure. Quilt a diamond shape in the center of the square using a zigzag stitch to join them together. Remove the pins. Trim excess batting and backing so block is 14" (35.5cm) square.

3. Fold ½" (1cm) lengthwise along both sides of the 2" x 14" (5cm x 35.5cm) strip of the pocket lining fabric and sew the folds down.

4. Place the strip flush along one edge of the quilt top layer of the pocket, right sides together, and sew along the edge. Turn the strip to the wrong side of quilt block and press in place.

5. Place the 14½" x 16½" (37cm x 42cm) fabric for pocket lining on top of the 14½" x 16½" (37cm x 42cm) backing fabric, right sides facing. Sew together around 3 sides, leaving 1 short side unsewn. Turn right side out and iron.

6. Place the quilt top pocket on top of the pocket lining, with right side of the quilt top facing the backing of the lining. Align the quilt top with the 3 sewn sides of the lining and sew them together, making sure not to join the side of the pocket that is sewn to the strip (Fig. 6). Trim the corners and turn the pocket right side out.

7. Place the large piece of batting on your worktable. Place the quilt top right side up

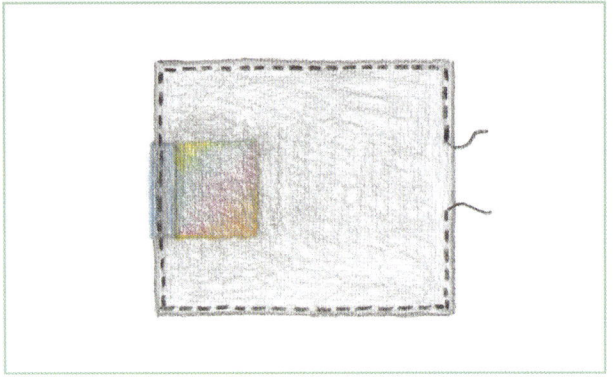

Fig. 7

on top of the batting and iron. Place the ironed and layered quilt top on top of the backing, right sides facing.

8. Tuck the unsewn short side of the quilt pocket between the layers at the center of the short side of the quilt. The backs and fronts of both pieces should be facing the same direction. (Fig. 7)

9. Join the pieces together and sew around all 4 sides, leaving a 5" (13cm) section unsewn at the bottom of the quilt. Make sure to secure the pocket in place.

10. Turn the quilt right side out and blindstitch the unsewn section.

Completing the Quilt

Follow Quilting (page 90) to mark, layer and complete the Quilt.

1. Quilt a zigzag stitch along the seams of the small squares only, to outline them. Do not stitch on the border. Sew horizontally and diagonally, moving from the center toward the outer edges to avoid distortion. Alternate between the turquoise and black threads to match the fabrics.

Gorgeous Garden Apron

This bright apron is made from several long strips of fabric in various shades of green. Though most of the strips are arranged vertically, I've positioned a few horizontally as well for contrast. This project isn't just great for using up fabric odds and ends - it's also a fantastic gift. After all, who doesn't have a good friend who loves puttering around in the kitchen!?

DIMENSIONS

* **Apron body:** 26" wide x 28" (66cm x 71cm) long
* **Straps:** Four strips ¾" x 18" (2cm x 46cm)

MATERIALS

* ¾ yard (68cm) of assorted green fabrics (scraps need to be at least 4½" (11cm) wide by various lengths, see cutting instructions)
* ¼ yard (23cm) of assorted pink fabrics (scraps need to be at least 4½" (11cm) wide by various lengths, see cutting instructions)
* ⅜ yard (34cm) of vibrant green, pink and black fabric
* ⅜ yard (34 cm) of matching green fabric for backing

BATTING

* 27" x 29" (69cm x 74cm) fusible batting

YOU WILL ALSO NEED

* Sheet of paper, 27" x 29" (69cm x 74cm)
* Pencil and scissors
* Multicolored bright thread

CUTTING THE PIECES

* Follow Rotary Cutting (page 87) to cut fabric. All measurements include ¼" (0.6cm) seam allowances.

FROM GREEN FABRICS

* Cut 3 strips 4½" x 15" (11cm x 38cm) each
* Cut 3 strips 4½" x 13" (11cm x 33cm) each
* Cut 3 strips 4½" x 9" (11cm x 23cm) each
* Cut 3 strips 4½" x 8" (11cm x 20cm) each
* Cut 3 strips 4½" x 7" (11cm x 18cm) each
* Cut 4 narrow strips 2½" x 20" (6.5cm x 51cm) each, for apron straps

FROM PINK FABRICS

* Cut 2 strips 4½" x 10" (11cm x 25cm) each
* Cut 2 strips 4½" x 9" (11cm x 23cm) each
* Cut 2 strips 4½" x 7" (11cm x 18cm) each

FROM VIBRANT GREEN, PINK AND BLACK FABRIC

* Cut 1 strip 3" x 13" (8cm x 33cm)
* Cut 1 strip 2½" x 13" (6cm x 33cm)
* Cut 1 square 10" x 10" for pocket (25cm x 25cm)

Assembling the Quilt Top

Follow directions for Machine Piecing (page 88) and Pressing (page 89) to sew pieces together.

1. Place a sheet of paper on your work surface and sketch an apron template that is 28" (71cm) long, 26" (66cm) wide (at the wide part) and 13" (33cm) wide (the narrow part). Allow for a ¼" (0.6cm) border along all sides and cut out template. (Fig. 1)

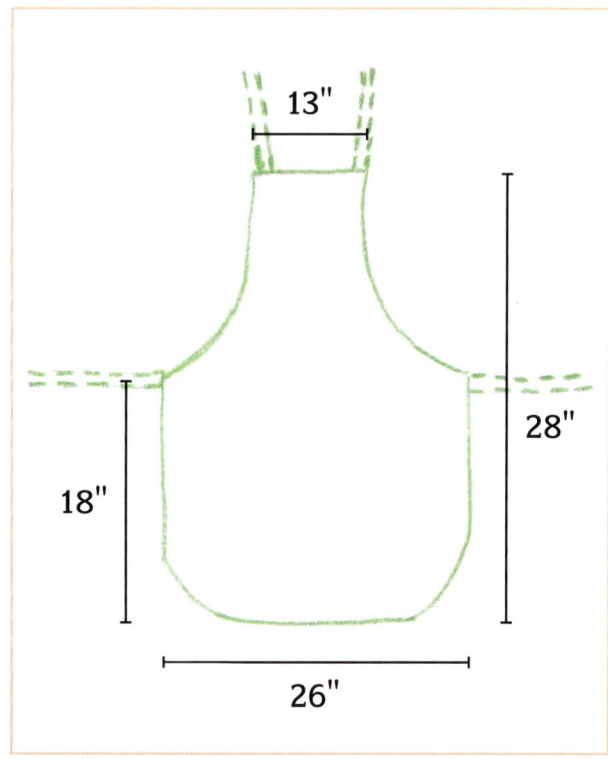

Fig. 1

2. Arrange the pink and green strips lengthwise on top of the template to cover the body and bib of the apron. (Fig. 2)

3. Sew together the sections of each new strip. Then sew the new strips together. Sew in opposite directions to avoid distortions. (Fig. 3)

4. Place the sewn fabric right side down on your work surface and trace the apron template. Cut out your apron quilt top.

Fig. 2

Assembling the Apron Straps

1. Fold each 2½" x 20" (6.5cm x 51cm) green fabric strip in half lengthwise, with right sides facing, and sew together along the length and across one short end.

2. Using a safety pin, turn each strip right-side out. These are your 4 apron straps.

Fig. 3

Completing the Quilt

Follow Quilting (page 90) to mark, layer and complete the quilt top.

1. Copy the template on a piece of batting and cut out.

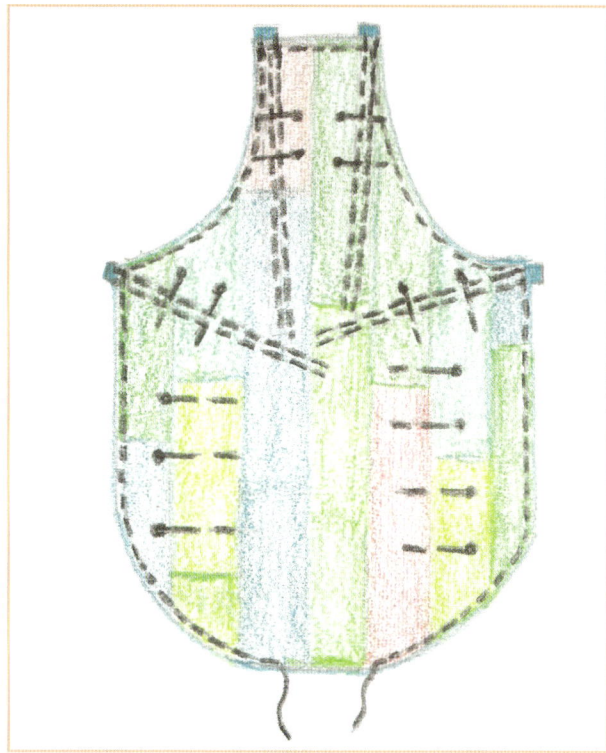

Fig. 4

2. Copy the template on backing fabric and cut out.

3. Place the cut batting piece on your ironing board. Place the apron quilt top right side up on top of apron shaped batting and iron to affix.

4. Place the backing on top, wrong side up so that the apron front and backing are right sides together.

5. Insert the unfinished ends of 2 straps at the top of the apron, at opposite ends, according to the illustration, between the backing and the apron top. Repeat with the other 2 straps, placing 1 strap at each side of the apron. (Fig. 4)

6. Pin the straps in place between the quilt layers to secure.

7. Sew around the apron from the bottom left corner upwards and around the top to the bottom right corner. Make sure to secure the straps as you sew. Leave a 4" (10cm) area along the bottom of the apron unsewn. Remove the pins.

8. Turn the apron right side out through the opening you left at the bottom of the apron. Blindstitch the opening closed.

(continued on page 74)

(continued from page 72)

9. Quilt the apron with a zigzag stitch along the lengthwise seams.

Adding the Finishing Touches

1. Fold the 10" x 10" (25cm x 25cm) vibrant fabric square in half, right sides facing. Sew together along three sides, leaving one short side open. Turn the fabric right side out to create the pocket for the quilt.

2. Fold the unsewn edge inside ½" (1.25cm) and press the fold. Pin the pocket to the quilted apron, folded under edge at the bottom of the apron. Sew the pocket to the apron with a zigzag stitch along the pocket's bottom and sides, making sure to secure it in place.

3. Place the 2 remaining 13" (33cm) strips of vibrant fabric on your ironing board, right side down. Fold fabric over ½" (1.25cm) on each side and iron in place. Place the strips right side up horizontally onto the apron front and zigzag around the edges as in step 2 to secure the strips.

Handy Hip Handbag

Create a stylish and sturdy handbag with leftover scraps from other projects. In this design, I've cut the blocks into diverse shapes and sizes to create a constellation of shapes. I worked with an assortment of fabrics in various shades of light green; some are smooth while others are brocade with gold thread. For the lining, I used printed green and black fabric. When quilting, I straight stitched with a multicolored green thread.

DIMENSIONS

* **Finished Quilted Handbag Size:** 14" x 14" (36cm x 36cm)
* **Block Size:** 5½" x 7¾" (14cm x 20cm)
* **Handle Size:** 2¼" x 29" (6cm x 74cm)

MATERIALS

* ⅝ yard (57cm) of solid green fabrics (scraps need to be at least 7" x 9" (18cm x 23cm)
* ½ yard (46cm) of brocade green fabrics (scraps need to be at least 7" x 9" (18cm x 23cm)
* ¾ yard (69cm) of green and black fabric for lining bag and handles

BATTING

* 2 pieces fusible batting, 16" x 16" (41cm x 41cm) each
* Batting for handles, 2 pieces fusible batting 2¾" x 29½" (7cm x 75cm) each

YOU WILL ALSO NEED

* Multicolored green thread

CUTTING THE PIECES

* Follow Rotary Cutting (page 87) to cut fabric. All measurements include ¼" (0.6cm) seam allowances.

FROM GREEN FABRICS

* Cut 11 rectangles 7" x 9" (18cm x 23cm) each, solid fabrics
* Cut 7 rectangles 7" x 9" (18cm x 23cm) each, from brocade fabrics

FROM GREEN WITH BLACK FABRIC

* Cut 1 wide piece 15" x 29" (38cm x 74cm)
* Cut 2 long strips 2¾" x 29½" (7cm x 75cm) each

Assembling the Quilt Top

Follow directions for Machine Piecing (page 88) and Pressing (page 89) to sew pieces together.

1. Place a 7" x 9" (18cm x 23cm) green fabric rectangle on your work surface and cut 6 sections as shown on the illustration. Repeat with all of the remaining rectangles. (Fig. 1)

2. Number each group of cut sections.

3. Rearrange the groups of sections to form new rectangles, using pieces from 6 different fabrics. (Fig. 2)

4. Sew the cut pieces of each rectangle together as follows: sew the 3 fabrics on the left side together and then sew together the

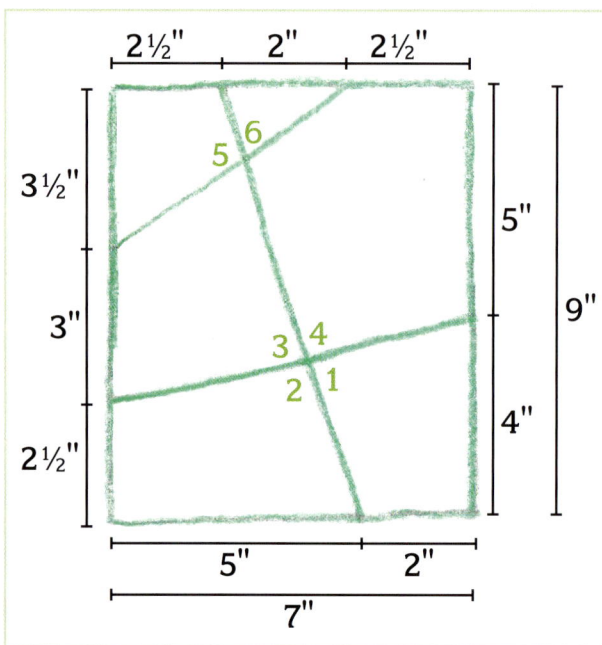

Fig. 1

Fig. 2

3 fabrics on the right side, finish by joining the 2 halves together. Trim all of the new rectangles to measure 5½" x 7¾" (14cm x 20cm) each.

5. Arrange 7 rectangles together to form a large square as shown in the illustration. Arrange the pieces to achieve an interesting pattern. Sew rectangles together. Trim the block to be 15" x 15" (38cm x 38cm). Repeat with other 7 rectangles. (Fig. 3)

6. Cut the remaining 4 rectangles in half, lengthwise, and sew 4 strips together to form a 2¾" x 29½" (7cm x 75cm) long strip. Repeat to make second handle.

Fig. 3

Completing the Quilt

Follow Quilting (page 90) to mark, layer and complete the quilt top.

1. Place 1 of the 2¾" x 29½" (7cm x 75cm) pieces of batting on your ironing board. Place a pieced handle, right side up, on the piece of batting and iron to affix. Repeat with the other piece of batting and pieced strap.

2. Place the pieced straps and the long strips of green with black fabric right sides

together and sew together along the long edges. Turn right side out.

3. Quilt along the seam lines joining the block pieces using a straight stitch.

4. Place 1 piece of 16" x 16" (41cm x 41cm) batting on your ironing board. Place a 15" x 15" (38cm x 38cm) quilt top square, right side up, on the batting and iron to affix. Repeat with the other pieces of batting and quilt top. Using a straight stitch, quilt both quilt top squares along seam lines in a random zig-zag fashion (see photo on page 79). Trim excess batting away so block is 15" (38cm) square.

5. Place the 2 quilt tops right sides facing and sew them together around 3 sides to create a pocket. Turn the pocket right side out.

6. Fold the 15" x 28" (38cm x 71cm) wide piece of green with black fabric in half, with right sides facing. Sew together along 3 sides, leaving a 4" (10cm) opening unsewn on 1 side. Do not turn.

7. Place the quilted handbag body right side out inside the lining, so that right sides of both are facing together. Match the top edges so they are even.

8. Insert 1 handle between the handbag and lining, with the lining of the handle facing the lining of the handbag. Place the handle ends on opposite sides, within 1" (2.5cm) from the edge, flush with the edges of both lining and handbag. Pin the fabrics together to secure. Repeat with the other handle on the opposite side of the handbag. (Fig. 4)

9. Sew along the top edge of the bag, double-stitching over the handles to secure them. Remove the pins.

10. Pull the bag through the opening in the side seam of the lining. Blindstitch the opening closed and tuck in the lining to finish your handbag.

Fig. 4

Practical Chair Pockets

Transform the back of an ordinary chair into a handy holder for maps, books, pens, and assorted odds and ends. Select leftover fabrics that are lively, fun and match the room where the chair will be located. You can even tie this to the back of the driver's seat in your car as an attractive way to store maps and other auto-related paraphernalia.

DIMENSIONS

* **Finished Quilt Size:** 10½" x 21" (26.5cm x 53cm)

YARDAGE REQUIREMENTS

* ⅜ yard (34cm) of various solid colored fabrics (scraps need to be at least 2" x 6¾" (5cm x 17cm))
* ¼ yard (23cm) of black with colored squares fabric (scraps need to be at least 6¾" x 6¾" (17cm x 17cm))
* ⅜ yard (34cm) of black with print fabric for pocket lining (piece needs to be at least 11" x 11" (28cm x 28cm))
* ⅜ yard (34cm) of matching purple fabric for backing

BATTING

* 11" x 32" (28cm x 81cm) fusible batting

YOU WILL ALSO NEED

* Multicolored thread to match the fabrics
* 4 black cords, 14" (35.5cm) long each

CUTTING THE PIECES

* Follow Rotary Cutting (page 87) to cut fabric. All measurements include ¼" (0.6cm) seam allowances.

FROM SOLID COLORED FABRICS

* Cut 18 strips 2" x 6¾" (5cm x 17cm) each or random sized strips which will be pieced together to make a strip set that is 6¾" x 27" (17cm x 68cm) each, long.

FROM BLACK WITH COLORED SQUARES FABRIC

* Cut 4 squares 6¾" x 6¾" (17cm x 17cm) each

FROM BLACK WITH PRINT FABRIC FOR LINING

* Cut 1 large square 11" x 11" (28cm x 28cm)

FROM BACKING FABRIC

* 11" x 32" (28cm x 81 cm) piece

Assembling the Quilt Top

Follow directions for Machine Piecing (page 88) and Pressing (page 89) to sew pieces together.

1. Arrange the solid colored fabric strips at random to make a strip set that is 6¾" x 27" (17cm x 68cm) long. Match the long edges of the strips and sew the seams in opposite directions to avoid distortion. (Fig. 1)

2. Cut the strip set to make 4 striped

Fig. 1

squares, each measuring 6¾" x 6¾" (17cm x 17cm).

3. Place 1 black with colored square fabric square on top of 1 striped square, right sides facing. Pin the squares together in the corners to hold them together and iron to compress. (Fig. 2)

Fig. 2

4. Place the square on your work surface, black side up, to prevent distortions. Draw a diagonal line between 2 opposite corners across the middle of the square.

5. Sew 2 seams along the diagonal line you drew in step 4, 1 seam on each side of the line. (Fig. 3)

Fig. 3

6. Cut the square into 2 equal triangles by cutting on the line between the diagonal seams. Press the triangles open. You have created 2 new squares, each with a diagonal seam across the center, connecting 1 black and 1 striped triangle. (Fig. 4)

7. Repeat steps 3—6 with the remaining 6½" x 6½" (16.5cm x 16.5cm) black and striped squares to create a total of 8 new squares. Trim new squares down to 5¾" x 5¾" (15cm x 15cm).

Fig. 4

8. Arrange 4 new squares to create 1 large square: My design shows 3 black and

Fig. 5

1 striped triangle sections at the center. Sew the squares together. (Fig. 5)

9. Repeat step 8 with the remaining 4 squares.

10. Place the large black with print design square, 11" x 11" (28cm x 28cm) between the 2 large squares you created. Sew them together to finish the 11" x 32" (28cm x 81cm) rectangle quilt top.

Completing the Quilt

Follow Quilting (page 90) to mark, layer and complete the Quilted Chair Pockets.

1. Place the batting piece on your work surface. Place the quilt top right side up on top of the batting and iron to affix.

2. Place the backing on your work surface, right side up. Place the quilt top with the batting on the backing, right side down. Tuck the ends of 2 black cords between the batting and backing next to a corner of one short end of the quilt (make sure the cords are contained inside the layers). Pin to secure. Repeat with the other 2 cords next to the other corner on the same short side.

Sew the three layers together all around the edges, leaving a 3" (8cm) opening unsewn. Double stitch over the cord ends to secure them in place.

3. Turn the quilt right side out and blindstitch closed the opening from step 2.

4. Quilt a zigzag stitch along some of the strips and seams.

5. Fold the sewn quilt in half in the middle so that the central square is turned into a pocket.

6. To finish, sew a lengthwise seam along the left and right sides of the folded section. Now sew a seam along the middle of the folded section to create 2 pockets. (Fig. 6)

Fig. 6

General Instructions

To make your quilting easier and more enjoyable, we encourage you to carefully read all of the general instructions, study the color photographs, and familiarize yourself with the individual project instructions before beginning a project.

FABRICS

Selecting Fabrics

Choose high-quality, medium-weight 100% cotton fabrics. All-cotton fabrics hold a crease better, fray less, and are easier to quilt than cotton/polyester blends.

The projects in this book were made using fabric scraps from the author's collection. The fabric requirements given in the project instructions are based on total fabric needed. If you wish to also use scraps, the minimum sizes for pieces are noted as well. Overall yardage requirements listed for each project are based on 43"/44" wide fabric with a 'usable' width of 40" after shrinkage and trimming selvages. Actual usable width will vary slightly from fabric to fabric.

Preparing Fabrics

We recommend that all fabrics be washed, dried, and pressed before cutting. If fabrics are not pre-washed, washing the finished quilt will cause shrinkage and give it a more 'antiqued' look and feel. Bright and dark colors, which may run, should always be washed before cutting. After washing and drying fabric, fold it lengthwise with wrong sides together and selvage edges matching.

ROTARY CUTTING

Rotary cutting has brought speed and accuracy to quiltmaking by allowing quilters to easily cut strips of fabric and then cut those strips into smaller pieces.

* Place folded fabric on work surface with fold closest to you.
* Cut all strips across the width of the fabric from fold to selvage unless otherwise indicated in project instructions.
* Square left edge of fabric using rotary cutter and rulers (Figs. 1 - 2).
* To cut each strip required for a project, place ruler over cut edge of fabric, aligning desired marking on ruler with cut edge; make cut (Fig. 3).
* When cutting several strips from a single piece of fabric, it is important to make sure that cuts remain at a perfect right angle to the fold; square fabric as needed.

Fig. 1

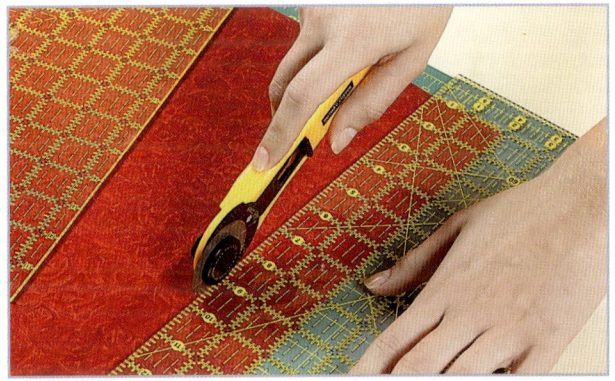

Fig. 2

Fig. 3

TEMPLATE CUTTING

Our piecing template patterns have two lines — a solid cutting line and a dashed line showing the ¼" seam allowance.

1. To make a template from a pattern, use a permanent fine-point pen and a ruler to carefully trace pattern onto template plastic, making sure to transfer any alignment and grain line markings. Cut out template along inner edge of drawn line.

Check template against original pattern for accuracy.

2. To use a template, place template face down on wrong side of fabric (unless otherwise indicated in project instructions), aligning grain line on template with straight grain of fabric. Use a sharp fabric-marking pencil to draw around template. Transfer all alignment markings to fabric. Cut out fabric piece using scissors or rotary cutting equipment.

PIECING AND PRESSING

Precise cutting, followed by accurate piecing, will ensure that all pieces of quilt top fit together well.

Hand Piecing

* Use ruler and sharp fabric marking pencil to draw all seam lines and transfer any alignment markings onto the back of cut pieces.
* Matching right sides, pin two pieces together, using pins to mark corners.
* Use a running stitch to sew pieces together along drawn line, backstitching at beginning and end of seam.
* Do not extend stitches into seam allowances.
* Run five or six stitches onto needle before pulling needle through fabric.
* To add stability, backstitch every ¾" to 1".

Machine Piecing

* Set sewing machine stitch length for approximately 11 stitches per inch.
* Use neutral-colored general-purpose sewing thread (not quilting thread) in needle and in bobbin.
* An accurate ¼" seam allowance is essential. Presser feet that are ¼" wide are available for most sewing machines.
* When piecing, always place pieces right sides together and match raw edges; pin if necessary.
* Chain piecing saves time and will usually result in more accurate piecing.
* Trim away points of seam allowances that extend beyond edges of sewn pieces.

Sewing Strip Sets

When there are several strips to assemble into a strip set, first sew strips together into pairs, then sew pairs together to form strip set. To help avoid distortion, sew seams in opposite directions (Fig. 4).

Sewing Across Seam Intersections

When sewing across intersection of two seams, place pieces right sides together and match seams exactly, making sure seam allowances are pressed in opposite directions (Fig. 5).

Sewing Sharp Points

To ensure sharp points when joining triangular or diagonal pieces, stitch across the center of the 'X' (shown in pink) formed on wrong side by previous seams (Fig. 6).

Pressing

Use steam iron set on Cotton for all pressing.

* Press after sewing each seam.
* Seam allowances are almost always pressed to one side, usually toward darker fabric. However, to reduce bulk it may occasionally be necessary to press seam allowances toward the lighter fabric or even to press them open.
* To prevent dark fabric seam allowance from showing through light fabric, trim darker seam allowance slightly narrower than lighter seam allowance.
* To press long seams, such as those in long strip sets, without curving or other distortion, lay strips across width of the ironing board.

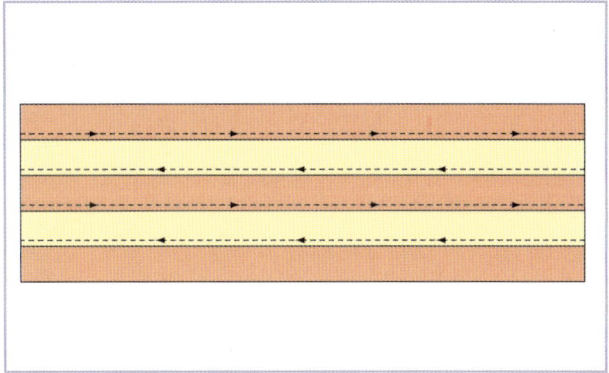

Fig. 4

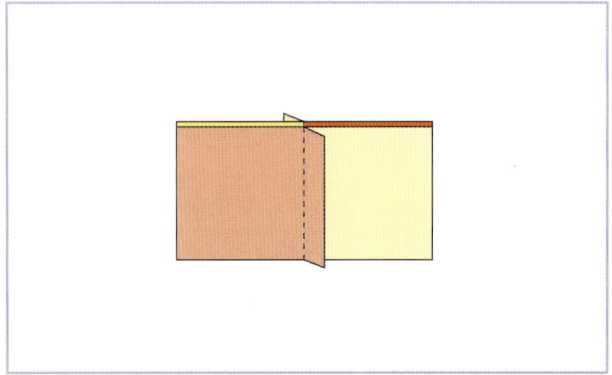

Fig. 5

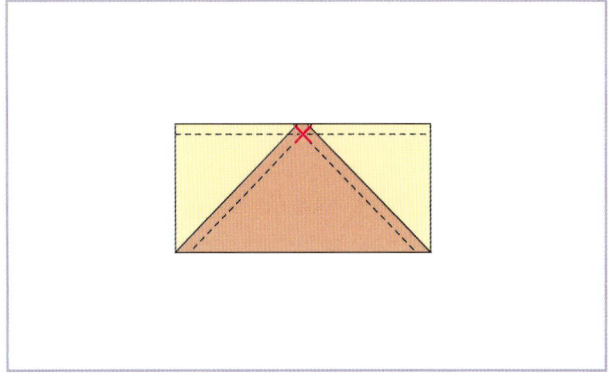

Fig. 6

BORDERS

Adding Squared Borders

In most cases, our instructions for cutting borders for bed-size quilts include an extra 2" of length at each end for 'insurance;' borders will be trimmed after measuring completed center section of quilt top.

1. Mark the center of each edge of quilt top.
2. Squared borders are usually added to top and bottom, then side edges of the center section of the quilt top. To add top and

bottom borders, measure across center of quilt top to determine length of borders. Trim top and bottom borders to the determined length.

3. Mark center of 1 long edge of top border. Matching center marks and raw edges, pin border to quilt top, easing in any fullness; stitch. Repeat for bottom border.

4. Measure center of quilt top, including attached borders, to determine length of side borders. Trim side borders to the determined length. Repeat Step 3 to add borders to quilt top.

QUILTING

Quilting holds the three layers (top, batting, and backing) of the quilt together and can be done by hand or machine. Because marking, layering, and quilting are interrelated and may be done in different orders depending on circumstances, please read entire Quilting section before beginning project.

Types of Quilting Designs

In the Ditch Quilting

Quilting along seam lines or along edges of appliquéd pieces is called 'in the ditch' quilting. This type of quilting should be done on side opposite seam allowance and does not have to be marked.

Outline Quilting

Quilting a consistent distance, usually ¼", from seam or appliqué is called 'outline' quilting. Outline quilting may be marked, or ¼" masking tape may be placed along seam lines for quilting guide. (Do not leave tape on quilt longer than necessary, since it may leave an adhesive residue.)

Channel Quilting

Quilting with straight, parallel lines is called 'channel' quilting. This type of quilting may be marked or stitched using a guide.

Crosshatch Quilting

Quilting straight lines in a grid pattern is called 'crosshatch' quilting. Lines may be stitched parallel to edges of quilt or stitched diagonally. This type of quilting may be marked or stitched using a guide.

Marking Quilting Lines

Quilting lines may be marked using fabric marking pencils, chalk markers or water- or air-soluble pens.

Simple quilting designs may be marked with chalk or chalk pencil after basting. A small area may be marked, and then quilted, before moving to next area to be marked. Intricate designs should be marked before basting using a more durable marker.

Caution: Pressing may permanently set

some marks. Test different markers on scrap fabric to find one that marks clearly and can be thoroughly removed.

A wide variety of pre-cut quilting stencils, as well as entire books of quilting patterns, are available. Using a stencil makes it easier to mark intricate or repetitive designs.

To make a stencil from a pattern, center template plastic over pattern and use a permanent marker to trace pattern onto plastic. Use a craft knife with single or double blade to cut channels along traced lines (Fig. 7).

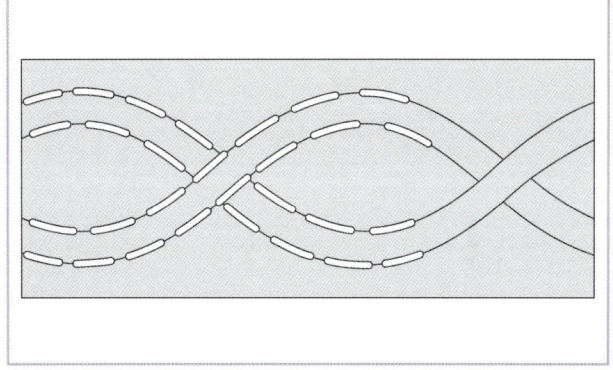

Fig. 7

Preparing the Backing

Yardage requirements listed for quilt backings are calculated for 43"/44" wide fabric. Using 90" wide or 108" wide fabric for the backing of a bed-sized quilt may eliminate piecing. To piece a backing using 43"/44" wide fabric, use the following instructions.

1. Measure length and width of quilt top; add 4" or 8" to each measurement, depending on the type of project.

2. If determined width is 79" or less, cut backing fabric into two lengths slightly longer than determined length measurement. Trim selvages. Place lengths with right sides facing and sew long edges together, forming tube (Fig. 8). Match seams

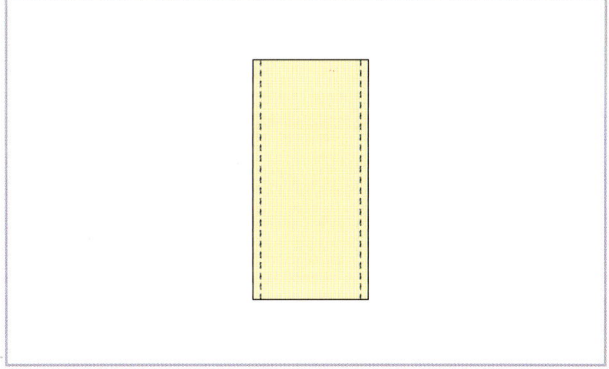

Fig. 8

and press along one fold (Fig. 9). Cut along pressed fold to form single piece (Fig. 10).
3. If determined width is more than 79", it may require less fabric yardage if the backing is pieced horizontally. Divide determined length measurement by 40" to determine how many widths will be needed. Cut required number of widths the determined width measurement. Trim selvages. Sew long edges together to form single piece.
4. Trim backing to size determined in Step 1; press seam allowances open.

Choosing the Batting

The appropriate batting will make quilting easier. For fine hand quilting, choose low-loft batting. All cotton or cotton/polyester blend battings work well for machine quilting because the cotton helps 'grip' quilt layers. If quilt is to be tied, a high-loft batting, sometimes called extra-loft or fat batting, may be used to make quilt 'fluffy.' Types of batting include cotton, polyester, wool, cotton/polyester blend, cotton/wool blend, and silk.

When selecting batting, refer to package labels for characteristics and care instructions. Cut batting same size as prepared backing.

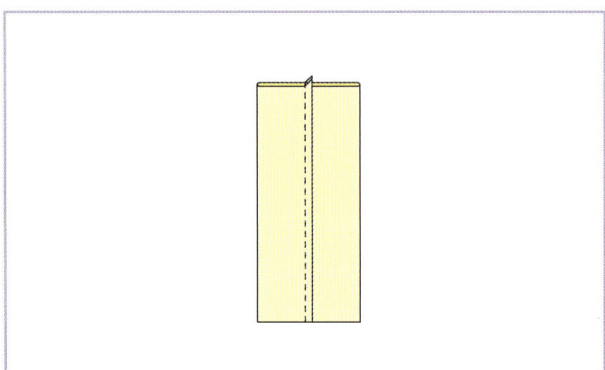

Fig. 9

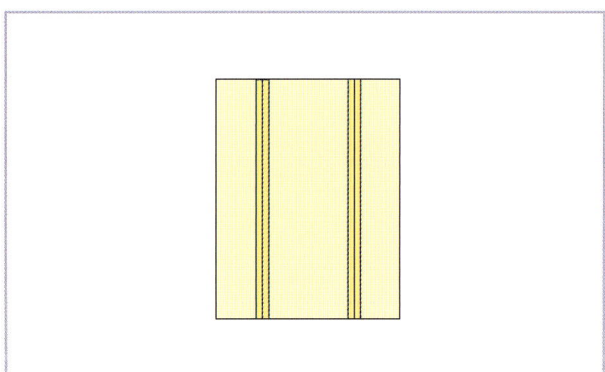

Fig. 10

Assembling the Quilt

1. Examine wrong side of quilt top closely; trim any seam allowances and clip any threads that may show through front of the quilt. Press quilt top, being careful not to 'set' any marked quilting lines.

2. Place backing wrong side up on flat surface. Use masking tape to tape edges of backing to surface. Place batting on top of backing fabric. Smooth batting gently, being careful not to stretch or tear. Center quilt top right side up on batting.

3. For machine quilting, use 1" rustproof safety pins to 'pin-baste' all layers together, spacing pins approximately 4" apart. Begin at center and work toward outer edges to secure all layers. If possible, place pins away from areas that will be quilted, although pins may be removed as needed when quilting.

Machine Quilting Method

Use general-purpose thread in bobbin. Do not use quilting thread. Thread the needle of machine with general-purpose thread or transparent monofilament thread to make quilting blend with quilt top fabrics. Use decorative thread, such as a metallic or multi-color general-purpose thread, to make quilting lines stand out more.

Straight-Line Quilting

The term 'straight-line' is somewhat deceptive, since curves (especially gentle ones) as well as straight lines can be stitched with this technique.

1. Set stitch length for six to ten stitches per inch and attach a walking foot to sewing machine.

2. Determine which section of quilt will have longest continuous quilting line, oftentimes area from center top to center bottom. Roll up and secure each edge of quilt to help reduce the bulk, keeping fabrics smooth. Smaller projects may not need to be rolled.

3. Begin stitching on longest quilting line, using very short stitches for the first ¼" to 'lock' quilting. Stitch across project, using one hand on each side of walking foot to slightly spread fabric and to guide fabric through machine. Lock stitches at end of quilting line.

4. Continue machine quilting, stitching longer quilting lines first to stabilize quilt before moving on to other areas.

5. Trim any excess backing and batting from quilt and square the edges of the quilt before sewing on the binding.

MAKING A HANGING SLEEVE

Attaching a hanging sleeve to the back of a wall hanging or quilt before the binding is added allows project to be displayed on wall.

1. Measure width of quilt top edge and subtract 1". Cut piece of fabric 7" wide by determined measurement.

2. Press short edges of fabric piece ¼" to wrong side; press edges ¼" to wrong side again and machine stitch in place.
3. Matching wrong sides, fold piece in half lengthwise to form tube.
4. Follow project instructions to sew binding to quilt top and to trim backing and batting. Before blindstitching binding to backing, match raw edges and stitch hanging sleeve to center top edge on back of quilt.
5. Finish binding quilt, treating hanging sleeve as part of backing.
6. Blindstitch bottom of hanging sleeve to backing, taking care not to stitch through to front of quilt.
7. Insert dowel or slat into hanging sleeve.

BINDING

Binding encloses the raw edges of quilt. Binding may be cut on the bias or from straight lengthwise or crosswise grain of fabric.

Making Straight-Grain Binding

1. Using diagonal seams (Fig. 11), sew binding strips together end to end to make 1 continuous binding strip.
2. Matching wrong sides and raw edges, press strip in half lengthwise.

Attaching Binding With Overlapped Corners

1. Matching raw edges and using ¼" seam allowance, sew a length of binding to top and bottom edges on right side of quilt.
2. If using 2½" wide binding (finished size ½"), trim backing and batting from top and bottom edges a scant ¼" larger than quilt top so that batting and backing will fill the binding when it is folded over to quilt backing. If using narrower binding, trim backing and batting even with edges of quilt top.
3. Trim ends of top and bottom binding even with edges of quilt top. Fold binding over to quilt backing and pin pressed edges in place, covering stitching line (Fig. 12); blindstitch binding to backing.
4. Leaving approximately 1½" of binding at each end, stitch a length of binding to each side edge of quilt. Trim backing and batting as in Step 2.
5. Trim each end of binding ½" longer than bound edge. Fold each end of binding over to quilt backing (Fig. 13); pin in place. Fold binding over to quilt backing and blindstitch in place, taking care not to stitch through to front of quilt.

SIGNING AND DATING YOUR QUILT

A completed quilt is a work of art and should be signed and dated. There are many different ways to do this and numerous books on the subject. The label should reflect the style of the quilt, the occasion or person for which it was made, and the quilter's own particular talents. Following are suggestions for recording the history of the quilt or adding a sentiment for future generations.

* Embroider quilter's name, date, and any additional information on quilt top or backing. Matching floss, such as cream floss on white border, will leave a subtle record. Bright or contrasting floss will make the information stand out.
* Make label from muslin and use permanent marker to write information. Use different colored permanent markers to make label more decorative. Stitch label to back of quilt.
* Use photo-transfer paper to add image to white or cream fabric label. Stitch label to back of quilt.
* Piece an extra block from quilt top pattern to use as label. Add information with permanent fabric pen. Appliqué block to back of quilt.
* Write message on appliquéd design from quilt top. Attach appliqué to back of the quilt.

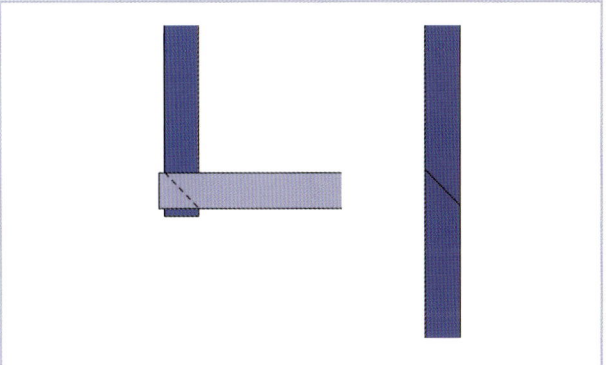

Fig. 11

Fig. 12

Fig. 13

HAND STITCHES
Blindstitch

Come up at 1, go down at 2, and come up at 3 (Fig. 14). Length of stitches may be varied as desired.

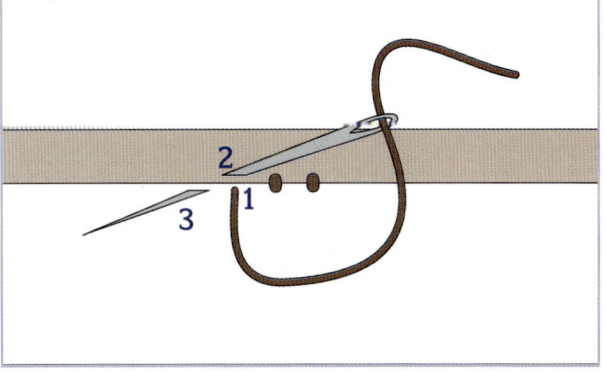

Fig. 14

Meet the Designer

Born on Kibbutz Yad Mordechai in southern Israel, Maya Chaimovich grew up in Holon, Israel, on the central coastal strip south of Tel Aviv. Today, she lives in Ramat Gan, east of Tel Aviv. Prior to developing her art in quilts, Chaimovich created all sorts of handiwork — from woodcarving, jewelry making, embroidery and needlepoint, to assorted weaving and lacework, in particular bobbin lace.

Her art quilts have been exhibited, and won recognition and awards, in her native country, as well as England, Japan, Switzerland, The Netherlands and the U.S. Her work also has appeared in numerous magazines and show catalogues. She has participated in the International Quilting Association exhibition, the Quilt Nihon Japan exhibition (2008 and 2010), and Quilt National in Athens, Ohio (2009). Maya solo exhibitions included MILESTONES in 2006 in Columbus, Ohio (USA) which traveled in 2007 to 5 different cities across England. Her current exhibition 'A Bundle of Letters' was exhibited in 2011 at the JCC in Columbus, Ohio and the JCC in Houston, Texas.

Metric Conversion Chart

Inches x 2.54 = centimeters (cm)
Inches x 25.4 = millimeters (mm)
Inches x .0254 = meters (m)

Yards x .9144 = meters (m)
Yards x 91.44 = centimeters (cm)
Centimeters x .3937 = inches (")
Meters x 1.0936 = yards (yd)

STANDARD EQUIVALENTS

⅛"	3.2mm	0.32cm
¼"	6.35mm	0.635cm
⅜"	9.5mm	0.95cm
½"	12.7mm	1.27cm
⅝"	15.9mm	1.59cm
¾"	19.1mm	1.91cm
⅞"	22.2mm	2.22cm
1"	25.4mm	2.54cm

⅛ yard	11.43cm	0.11m
¼ yard	22.86cm	0.23m
⅜ yard	34.29cm	0.34m
½ yard	45.72cm	0.46m
⅝ yard	57.15cm	0.57m
¾ yard	68.58cm	0.69m
⅞ yard	80cm	0.8m
1 yard	91.44cm	0.91m